DANGEROUS ANIMALS
SURVIVAL GUIDE

Acknowledgements

Dedicated to my favourite animals, my family – Louisa, Ella and Sophie.

Also, to my reading buddy, Harley – good call on including the King Cobra. We saved the best for last.

Collins

DANGEROUS ANIMALS
SURVIVAL GUIDE

By wildlife filmmaker
Sam Hume

About the author

Hi, I'm Sam, the author of this book! When I'm not writing, I make wildlife programmes for TV. I've been lucky enough to travel around the world and work with brilliant people like Steve Backshall, Andy Day and Sir David Attenborough. Most of the time, though, I work with camera teams and scientists to record amazing animals. I've filmed lions, sharks, bears, crocodiles, snakes, scorpions... the list goes on and on.

The most important part of my job is keeping everyone safe, especially when working around dangerous animals. It's not always easy. I've been charged by a bear, bitten by a lion cub, wrestled by an orangutan, and suckered by an octopus – here's the proof!

For all the scratches, stings, cuts and bruises, I'm pleased to say that I've never had a serious injury from any animal, despite a lifetime of working with them – which is largely thanks to the survival tips I've followed along the way.

Are you ready to meet the world's deadliest animals?

You're about to discover 50 of the most fascinating and fearsome creatures on our planet. You'll find out how these animals behave; see where they live in the world; learn to speak their language; discover the early-warning signs of an attack; and find out what to do if the worst happens.

While many of you will probably never come face-to-face with these awesome creatures in the wild, it's important to understand how they live and hunt. For those who *do* live near them, knowing how to stay safe is essential. The real-life survival tips you'll find in this book can help people to protect themselves in case they encounter these creatures.

It's true that animals can be dangerous, even deadly, but most of the time they just want to stay safe and avoid any problems. The best way to protect them *and* us is to respect these creatures and their homes. By leaving them undisturbed in their natural habitats, we can help to ensure that they thrive and continue to be a part of our world.

So, get ready to meet these incredible animals and discover the ways they survive in the wild!

Shapes and sizes

As you'll see in this book, every animal has a biological classification, which is based on their shared characteristics. Remember, dangerous animals come in all different shapes and sizes. Some might not even look or sound that scary at first, but don't let that fool you...

Mammals — Animals that are hairy, warm-blooded and make milk to feed their babies, like humans.

Amphibians — Animals that can live both on land and in water, like frogs and toads.

Fish — Cold-blooded animals that live in water and can breathe underwater using gills.

Birds — Animals with feathers and wings. Most birds can fly, and female birds lay eggs.

Invertebrates — Animals that don't have a backbone, like worms, beetles, crabs and jellyfish.

Reptiles — Cold-blooded animals that have scales and lay eggs, like snakes, lizards and crocodiles.

Status in the wild

Despite their fearsome reputations, some dangerous animals are struggling, which you'll see in their 'status' – a scientific label that sums up how the animals are doing in their fight for survival. Some are doing well, and their numbers might even be going up, while others are close to 'extinction', which is a word for when there are no more of those animals left at all. Most of the animals in this book fall into these categories...

Unknown ☐ ? ☐ ? ☐

There isn't enough information to know how the animal is doing – either because nobody has studied it or their home is too difficult to explore.

Least concern ■■■■■

There are large numbers of the animal and it is spread over a large area.

Near-threatened ■■■■☐

An animal might be close to needing our help, because numbers are dropping or their home is shrinking.

Vulnerable ■■■☐☐

There is a high chance of the animal going extinct in the wild.

Endangered ■■☐☐☐

There is a very high chance of the animal going extinct in the wild.

Critically endangered ■☐☐☐☐

The animal is incredibly close to extinction and needs urgent attention.

Grassland
page 12

Water
page 50

Desert
page 88

Frozen
page 124

Jungle
page 150

Wild Weapons
page 180

Grassland

With so much grass to eat, you'd think life here would be easy... but it's packed with danger. With few places to hide, both hunters and hunted must be super sneaky, lightning fast, or ready to stand and fight.

African Lion

|||| Grassland

◻ Mammal

very strong!

large claws

The 'king of the jungle' has a fearsome reputation. Rippling with muscles, lions weigh twice as much as adult humans, have razor-sharp claws and ten-centimetre-long, dagger-like teeth.

Lions are the only big cats that live in a family group, or a 'pride'. By hunting together, they can tackle massive prey such as giraffes, buffalo and even young elephants, though wildebeest and antelopes are more commonly on the menu.

Attacks on humans are very unusual and are often carried out by sick or old lions that are unable to hunt their normal prey. Though rare, lion attacks can be deadly, causing between 200 and 250 human deaths per year.

Method of attack

Lions rely on being sneaky to hunt, hoping they don't get spotted as they try and get close enough to attack. They stalk their prey quietly and carefully through long grasses or under the cover of darkness. Once in strike range, they sprint and tackle their prey before delivering a killer bite to the neck.

STORMY STEALTH

Lions like to hunt during storms. The sound of wind, rain and thunder makes it harder for their prey to hear them coming.

How to stay alive

✗ **NEVER RUN FROM A LION.** Running is something their prey does, and it will trigger them to chase you! Lions can run at around 80 kilometres per hour, twice as fast as Usain Bolt, so you'll never win that race! As one guide put it, 'You'll just die tired.' Instead, keep facing them and slowly back away into the nearest vehicle, building or tent.

✓ **LET THE LION KNOW YOU'VE SEEN IT.** Keep your eyes locked on it, wave your arms and shout your head off. When they know they've lost the element of surprise, they often give up.

✗ **NEVER TURN YOUR BACK ON A LION.** If you turn your back, the lion will sprint towards you while it knows you can't see it.

✗ **DON'T WALK AT NIGHT IN LION COUNTRY.** Lions have incredible night vision – eight times better than our own. Lions mostly hunt at night and sleep during the day.

STATUS

Vulnerable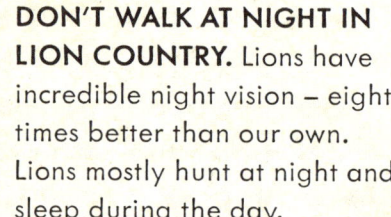

Despite their deadly reputation, lions are struggling to survive. Targeted by poachers and poisoned by cattle ranchers, there are now just 20,000 lions in all of Africa. If all those lions sat in the average football stadium, they'd only fill half the seats!

- **WEAR RED.** Lions around Kenya and Tanzania seem to keep their distance from the colour red. This might be because local Maasai warriors, who hunt lions, wear red.

- **STAY INSIDE THE VEHICLE!** If you're lucky enough to see a wild lion, then chances are you're on safari. Provided you're inside a vehicle, you should be perfectly safe to enjoy these awesome hunters from the sidelines.

- **MAKE THEM SCARED OF YOU!** Lions are very afraid of being injured. So turn the tables and make them scared of you! Throwing sticks or stones, shouting, pretending to charge them, or threatening them with a long stick might make them think twice.

Black Rhino

|||| Grassland

▫ Mammal

It wouldn't be wise to get too close to any kind of rhino when it's grumpy, but the most aggressive is the black rhino. Weighing 1,000 kilograms, it weighs as much as a small car. On its head are two large horns, which can grow over a metre long and end in a very sharp point – dangerous enough to keep lions at bay.

Black rhinos are badly named because they're usually grey. A good way to tell them apart from white rhinos is their pointy top lip, which is used to pluck leaves from their favourite plants.

Method of attack

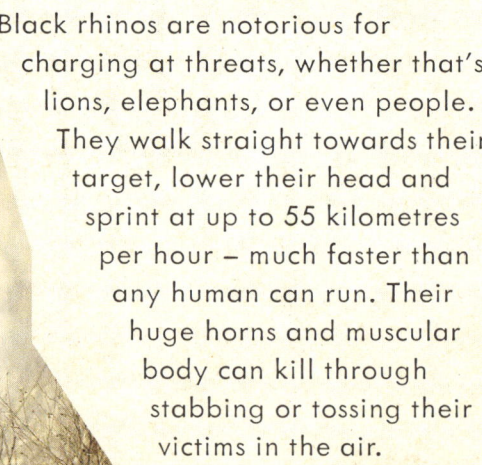

Black rhinos are notorious for charging at threats, whether that's lions, elephants, or even people. They walk straight towards their target, lower their head and sprint at up to 55 kilometres per hour – much faster than any human can run. Their huge horns and muscular body can kill through stabbing or tossing their victims in the air.

How to stay alive

+ **KEEP YOUR DISTANCE.** If you give rhinos plenty of space, they should stay calm. If they walk towards you, move backwards.

✓ **LEARN TO SPEAK RHINO.** A loud snort and ears lying flat against its back can indicate an angry rhino.

↓ **STAY IN THE VEHICLE.** Black rhinos can charge a car, but it's still your best bet for a quick exit, and you're unlikely to be hurt if you stay inside one.

✱ **ALWAYS BE PREPARED.** Stay ready to make a fast exit. Rhinos have very bad eyesight and will sometimes charge any large shape nearby if they're feeling frightened. They've even been known to charge at termite mounds and trees by mistake.

● **LOOK OUT FOR ALARMING BEHAVIOUR.** Rhinos sometimes react to the alarm calls of other animals nearby and start panicking. Pay attention to the behaviour of all the surrounding wildlife.

STATUS

Critically endangered ◼︎☐☐☐☐

There are only around 6,400 black rhinos left in the wild, mostly because poachers kill them to take their magnificent horns. Some people mistakenly believe these can be used as medicine, but they are actually made of the same stuff as your fingernails and hair.

Hippopotamus

||||| Grassland

▫ Mammal

50-centimetre teeth!

not-so-gentle giant

The hippopotamus (or simply 'hippo') might fool you into thinking it's friendly with its big smile, wiggly ears, and vegetarian diet. In reality, the hippo is one animal you really don't want to cross. At 2,000 kilograms, these enormous creatures weigh as much as a car, and can run at 30 kilometres per hour. Armed with some of the biggest teeth in the animal kingdom, they can bite down three times harder than a lion. Each year, hippos kill as many as 500 people – that's a lot more than lions!

Despite their size, hippos are nervous creatures with bad eyesight, so are easily spooked into getting defensive. They are also very territorial – which means they like to protect their home area and their family. During the day, they're usually found in or under the water trying to keep out of the sun. They often hang around in large groups called a 'bloat'. These groups can include as many as 200 hippos!

Method of attack

Hippos often live in muddy waterholes and rivers where the brown water makes it hard to spot them. People in kayaks and boats don't realise hippos are waiting just beneath the water until suddenly, in an explosive charge, they rocket towards the intruder like a missile. They can flip boats and even bite them in two.

STINKY SWEAT

The skin of hippos produces its own special red goo known as blood sweat, which acts like a sunscreen. Before you try and use some, be warned — it smells terrible!

How to stay alive

- **KEEP YOUR DISTANCE.** Give hippos plenty of space and remember there may be one underwater that you can't see.

- **HIDE AND DON'T SEEK.** Avoid dense thickets of grass or bushes. During the dry season, hippos may not have water to hide in and will often be in dense clusters of trees.

- **MAKE SOME NOISE.** If you're kayaking, routinely tap the side of your boat to let them know you're there, which should reduce the chances of them coming up beneath you.

- **KNOW YOUR BIRD CALLS.** Hippos often have oxpecker birds on them that pick out ticks and parasites. If you hear an oxpecker, chances are there's something big nearby.

- **SEEK COVER.** Unlike some of the other animals in this book, making yourself big or shouting is unlikely to stop a hippo in its tracks. Get something between you and the hippo, like a tree or a vehicle.

STATUS

Vulnerable ☐☐☐☐☐

There are roughly 120,000 hippos in Africa today, which sounds like a big number, but they are under pressure. Hippos are sometimes hunted for their meat, or for their teeth which can be used in making jewellery. These water lovers often compete with humans for the same water, which can lead to some animals losing their homes or even getting killed.

Giraffe

bony horns

loooong neck

| Grassland

◻ Mammal

When you see a giraffe from far away, it can look almost dainty with its thin, spindly legs and little head. Yet as they come nearer and the ground trembles under hooves as big as dinner plates, you start to realise the true size of them. Reaching almost six metres high, they are the tallest land creatures. Even newborn giraffes are taller than most grown men.

Method of attack

When giraffes feel nervous or threatened, they might treat you like a predator. Their kick is powerful enough to kill a lion or hyena, and they normally aim for the head. The hard 'horns' (known as 'ossicones') on their head are made of bone. Male giraffes will swing these into each other when competing for a mate. Giraffe attacks on people are extremely rare, but when they do happen, they can be deadly.

LONG LICKER

At 50 centimetres long, a giraffe's purple tongue is so big it can clean its own ears. It uses that tongue to reach leaves in thorny trees.

How to stay safe

✓ **BE CALM.** Avoid making loud noises or sudden movements.

● **READ THE BODY LANGUAGE.** A giraffe that's feeling threatened will stare at you and show you its weapons by stomping its feet or swinging its head.

↑ **KEEP YOUR DISTANCE.** Especially from a mother protecting her calf.

+ **WATCH OUT FOR THOSE LEGS.** Giraffes can kick with both their front and back legs, and they will reach further than you expect.

✳ **MIND THE HEAD.** Although their horns are only around 15 centimetres long, giraffes have such heavy skulls that when they swing their heads it's like a spiky wrecking ball, and can be deadly.

STATUS

Vulnerable ☐☐☐☐☐

Giraffe numbers have gone down by more than a third in the last 30 years, and sadly that decline seems to be continuing. Some of the reasons are humans building over their habitats, farming their land and removing the trees they rely on for food.

African Elephant

|||| Grassland

◻ Mammal

two-metre tusks

very heavy!

This animal needs no introduction. These are the biggest land animals in the world and everything about them is massive. The shoulders of big males (or 'bulls') are over twice the height of a man. They can weigh up to 6,000 kilograms – that's more than 100 children. Even their ears are the size of umbrellas.

African elephants usually live in tight-knit family herds, led by an older female. This 'matriarch' (pronounced *may-tree-arc*) has the experience needed to find food and water. You may have heard the saying 'elephants never forget' – they certainly do have an amazing memory. They can remember every waterhole over huge distances and in a drought can travel in a straight line to the nearest water, even if it's 50 kilometres away.

Method of attack

Despite their mostly slow and easy-going nature, these big beasts can quickly turn from 'ele-fun-t' to 'ele-not-so-fun-t'! When they want to, elephants can charge at 24 kilometres per hour. Flinging their tusks around and grabbing with their trunk, they generally maul and crush their victims or impale them with their tusks.

Elephants can attack for all sorts of reasons, often to protect themselves or their herd. When bull elephants come into 'musth', they are especially dangerous. Musth is when they're trying to impress females by picking fights and throwing their considerable weight around.

TREMENDOUS TRUNKS

The human body has 650 muscles; an elephant's trunk has 40,000!

How to stay alive

↑ **KEEP YOUR DISTANCE.** Treat elephants like the celebrities they are and admire them from afar!

● **WATCH OUT FOR WEE!** Bull elephants in musth often dribble urine. That's a dangerous elephant.

✗ **HEAD SHAKE MEANS NO.** When an elephant shakes its head, swings its trunk and flaps its ears, it's trying to warn you off. Take the hint!

✳ **LOOK FOR A WAGGING TAIL.** Like a dog, if an elephant is swishing away flies with its tail, it's probably quite relaxed. If it goes stiff, it's on alert.

🌀 **LOOK INTO THEIR EYES.** Like humans, if an elephant's eyes are half-closed, then they're probably relaxed. Wide eyes mean they might be nervous.

✓ **STEP ASIDE.** Elephants often don't like people being directly in their path.

✗ **BEWARE THE TRUMPETS.** Despite what you hear in movies, elephants rarely trumpet. If they do, it's a sign of distress and time to clear out.

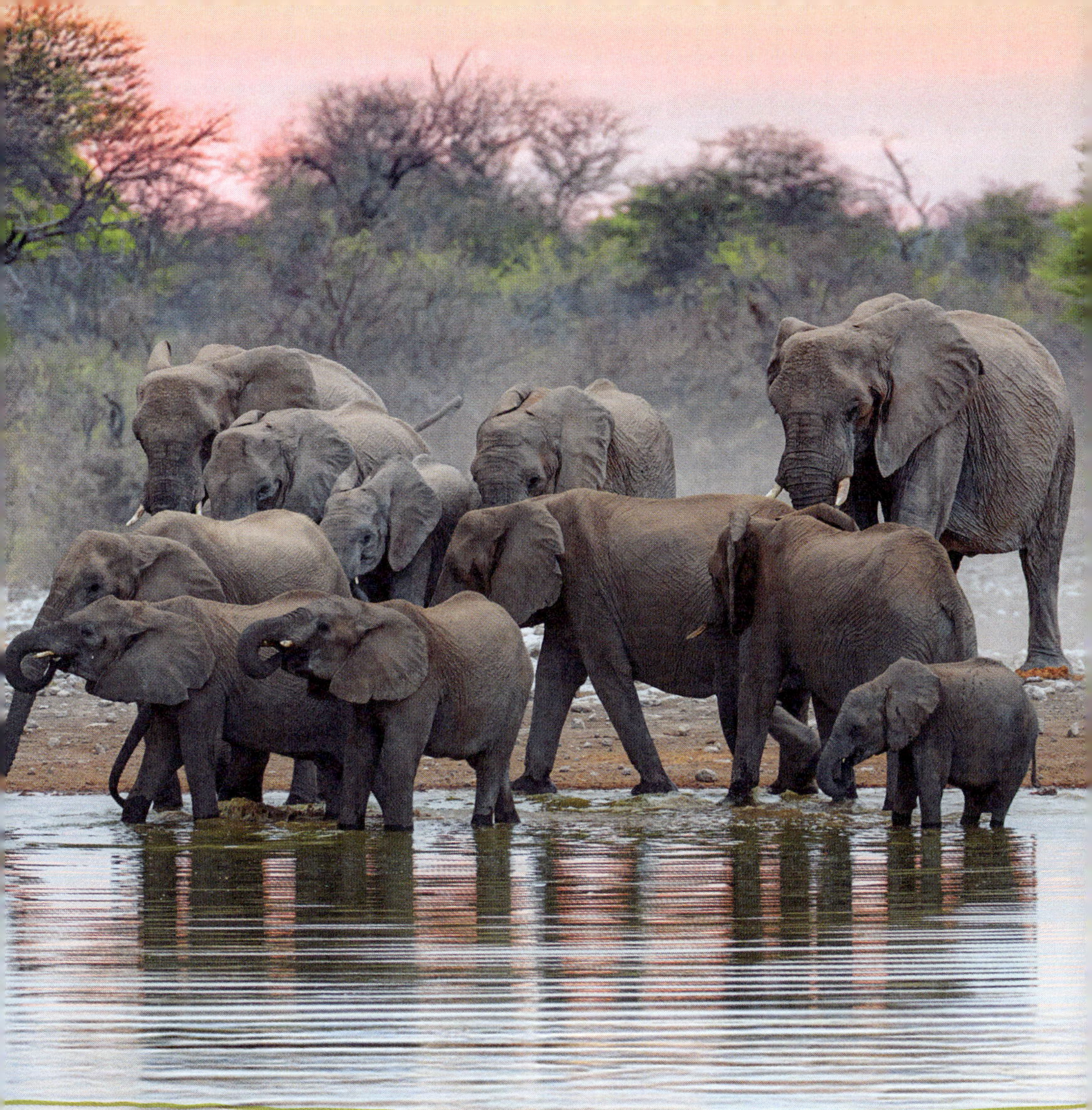

Endangered 🟧⬜⬜⬜⬜

African elephants used to be found throughout Africa. Now, sadly, their numbers are decreasing. Threats include: being hunted for their tusks, and for trophies; being killed by farmers trying to protect their crops; and their homes shrinking as human towns and cities expand.

Cattle

| Grassland
| Mammal

looooong horns

mega muscles

A regular 'cow' might seem like a surprising animal to have in this book alongside lions and crocodiles, but each year cattle kill dozens of people around the world, and injure thousands more, giving them a worse track record than sharks. Just like dogs have different breeds, cattle come in a variety of shapes and sizes. The largest is the Chianina which can grow over two metres tall, with bulls (older males) able to weigh up to 1,500 kilograms. That's as much as a car! Most varieties of cattle also have horns. Some – like the famous Texas longhorns – can have horns as long as a person, with a nasty-looking point.

COUNTING COWS

There are around one and a half billion cattle in the world – that's roughly one for every five people.

Method of attack

The main reason cattle are dangerous is because of all that weight that they can throw around. Most people injured are farmers, who might get crushed against a wall or trampled on. When they're feeling threatened, cattle will use their thick skull as a battering ram and their horns to stab at the threat.

How to stay safe

↑ **KEEP YOUR DISTANCE.** Cattle are normally easy to avoid as they're almost always penned in. If you don't have to go through a field with cattle, then don't!

✓ **STICK TO THE PATH.** The most likely time you'll come face to face with cattle is in a field with a footpath. Cows will be used to people passing through and will probably mind their own business.

◉ **TRY NOT TO SCARE THEM.** Despite their size, cattle are often scaredy-cats. Young animals in particular can be quick to spook. Make slow, steady movements.

+ **TALK TO THEM.** You don't want to surprise cattle; a friendly bit of chatter will let them know you're there.

+ **HOLD YOUR NERVE.** Cattle are curious. They might look at you or even approach. Just keep on walking slowly or stand still and let them believe that you're not very interesting!

✳ **APPLAUD THEM.** Clapping your hands together and making a noise can encourage them to leave you alone.

✗ **DO NOT RUN.** As well as curious and quick to spook, cattle can be playful. If you suddenly start running, there's a good chance they will too.

● **WATCH OUT FOR MUM.** Cows are great mothers and will try to protect their calves. Be sure not to come between a mum and her little one.

STATUS

Least concern 🟩🟩🟩🟩

Farm animals tend to have different problems than wild animals who are just trying to survive. We're experts at keeping cattle alive. However, they don't always have the best lives — some are kept in tiny, dirty spaces. If you eat beef or drink cow's milk, try to find out where it's come from. Ideally a farm with lots of space and time outdoors in nature.

Brown Bear

|||| Grassland

▢ Mammal

strong jaw

slashing claws

Prowling the northern wilderness of Asia, Europe and North America are the mighty brown bears. They can weigh up to 600 kilograms, as heavy as eight people. Standing at almost two-and-a-half metres tall, they would tower over even the tallest basketball players. Most of the time these giants graze on grasses, nuts and berries but when they need to, they turn into mega meat-eaters.

Brown bears are top predators and hunt everything from salmon and musk ox, to moose and caribou. Living in the high north, they hibernate through cold winters. To pile on the pounds before their winter sleep, they need to eat a lot – the equivalent of 80 cheeseburgers a day!

Method of attack

Brown bears have an extraordinary sense of smell – 2,000 times better than ours – detecting food from three kilometres away. They can run at almost 50 kilometres per hour to chase down their prey before catching it with ten-centimetre-long curved claws, on paws the size of dinner plates. Their powerful jaws deliver the killer blow. Brown bears are excellent climbers and swimmers; their prey doesn't have much hope of escape. Attacks on humans are rare but when they happen, they can be deadly.

How to stay alive

* **TALK TO YOURSELF.** Bears will normally try to avoid people, so let them know you're there by constantly making sounds.

* **STAY CALM.** Talking in a calm voice and moving slowly will let the bear know you don't mean any harm.

* **NEVER FEED BEARS.** They will start to think of humans as a place to find food, and it can lead to them getting too close for comfort.

* **AVOID CUBS.** Bears sometimes leave their cubs alone while they hunt. If you see a cub, the mum will be close and she won't want a babysitter.

* **DON'T RUN.** Brown bears are the fastest bears on Earth, easily outrunning an Olympic sprinter. Running might make them chase you.

* **MAKE YOURSELF BIG.** Open your coat, put your hands above your head. Try to look scary.

* **DON'T CLIMB A TREE.** Brown bears are excellent climbers, so it won't be a safe place to hide.

* **CARRY BEAR SPRAY.** Only use it if you absolutely have to, but a hit of bear spray should send that sensitive nose packing.

* **DON'T DROP YOUR BACKPACK.** It might give your back protection from their massive claws if it does attack.

* **PLAY DEAD.** A protective mother might be satisfied that the threat to her cubs is over.

* **DEFEND YOURSELF.** If playing dead doesn't stop the attack, then defend yourself by punching, kicking and throwing stones.

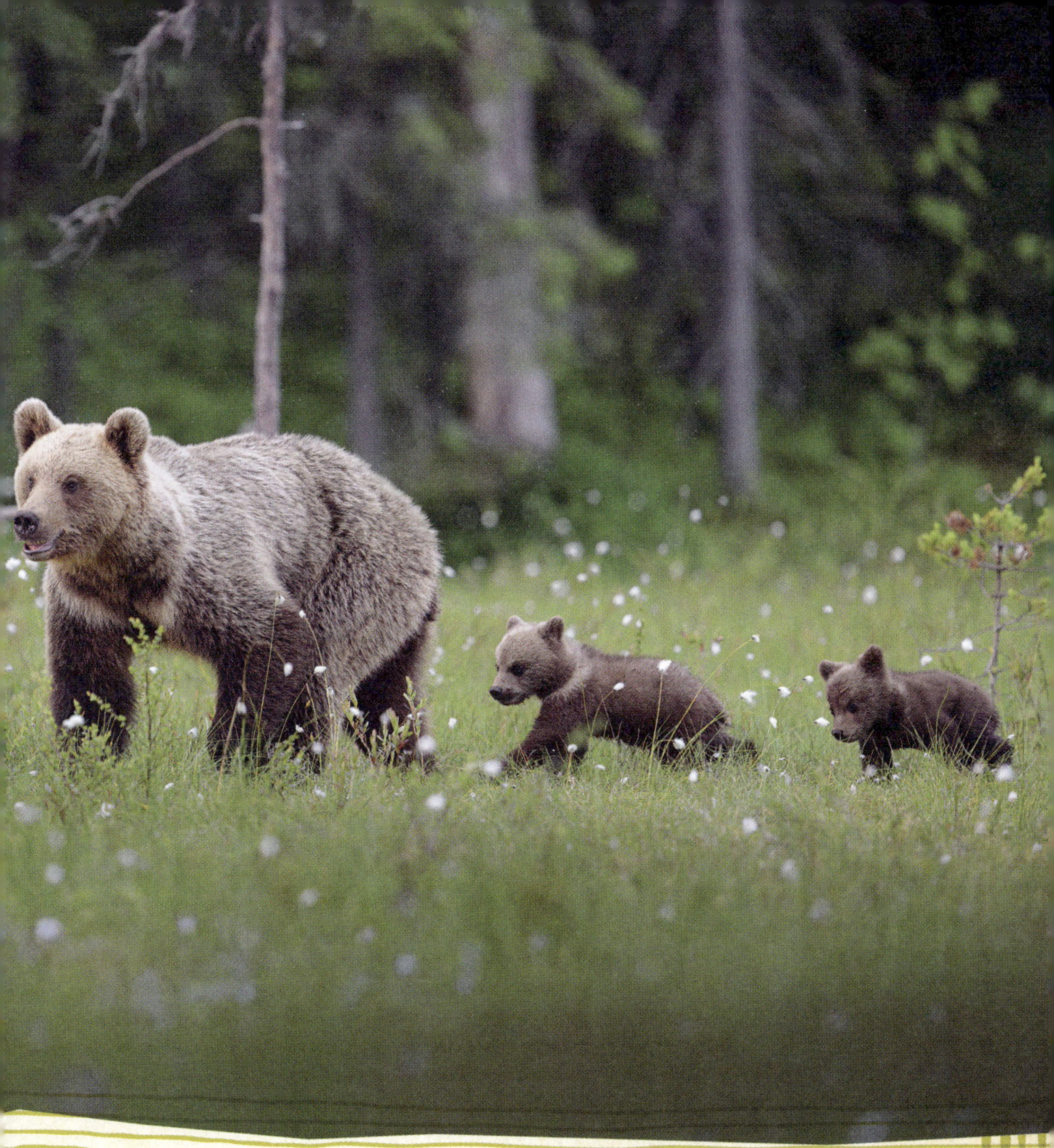

STATUS

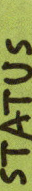

Least concern

Brown bears are widespread and mostly doing well, with numbers even increasing in some parts of the world. However, in Europe they still need a lot of protection in areas where they come into contact with humans.

Mosquito

Grassland

Invertebrate

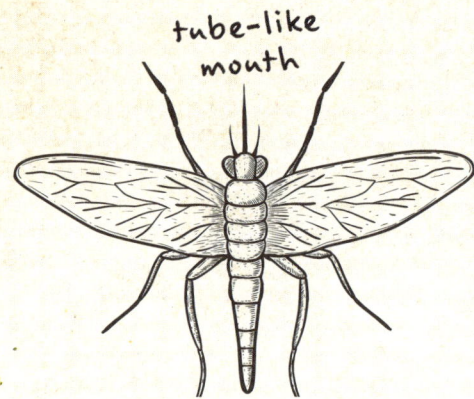

tube-like mouth

disease carriers

Mosquitoes are one of the least popular animals in the world and for good reason. These blood-sucking flies have a nasty habit of finding any bare skin, sneakily taking a drink, and leaving you with an unbelievably itchy spot as they fly off to find another victim. Even the whine of their tiny wings flapping is enough to keep you awake at night. Worst of all, some mosquitoes don't just take blood, they also leave something behind – diseases.

Mosquitoes are the deadliest animals in the world because they can spread serious illnesses such as malaria. With each bite, they can suck up a disease from one person and pass it onto the next. It's thought mosquitoes infect well over 300 million people with diseases every year and cause over 700,000 deaths. While mosquitoes can be found all over the world, the diseases they spread are normally found in tropical areas.

Method of attack

Mosquitoes have amazing senses to help them find blood. They can detect your breath from ten metres away. As they get closer, they can smell your sweat. From 70 centimetres away, they can follow your heat. Finally, when they land, they taste your skin with their feet to decide where to bite. Their pointy mouths have six incredibly thin needles. Two have saw-like teeth to cut through the skin, two hold the skin apart, one needle injects its special saliva which gets the blood flowing, and one is like a drinking straw to suck it up.

FIERCE FEMALES

Only female mosquitoes bite humans; males much prefer flower nectar.

How to stay alive

✓ **COVER UP YOUR SKIN.** Wear long sleeves, trousers and socks.

+ **SLAP, DON'T SCRATCH.** Slapping bites can help with the itchiness and it doesn't damage your skin.

✱ **USE CANDLES AND FIRES.** Smoke from candles and fires messes with mosquito senses and tends to keep them away.

+ **GET IN A NET.** You can get mosquito nets to go around your bed or even hang off your hat. The tiny mesh means mosquitoes can't get through. These are usually cheap, easy to buy and nice gifts to leave behind for people who need them most.

✱ **TAKE MEDICINE.** Mosquitoes are so good at finding us that sometimes it's easier to just worry about stopping the diseases they spread. Taking medicine, like antimalarial tablets, can help to ensure you don't catch a disease even if you do get bitten.

✓ **USE MOSQUITO SPRAY.** There are many different bug sprays out there, all acting to block the mosquito's clever senses.

◎ **MOISTURISE.** Sometimes, perfumed moisturising skin cream can work even better than bug spray. Even the Royal Marine Commandos use it!

STATUS

Increasing 🟩🟩➕➕🟩

Mosquitoes love warm, wet weather and as the world heats up through climate change, we're starting to see them in areas that used to be too cold for them. Not all mosquitoes carry deadly diseases. Most don't cause us harm and are important food for other animals.

Honey Badger

- Grassland
- Mammal

powerful bite!

sharp claws

Although their name sounds sweet, honey badgers are one of the most aggressive animals in this book. They only weigh around ten kilograms – about three times the size of a house cat – but with a sharp, powerful bite, and a jaw that can lock shut, they are not to be messed with.

They have very thick, loose skin which is excellent protection. If a predator bites them, they can spin around in their baggy skin and bite them back. It's like wearing a furry leather jacket. Being able to stand up to bigger animals makes them incredibly confident. They can attack people and have even been known to charge a whole pride of lions.

Method of attack

Honey badgers can walk over 20 kilometres a day, hoping to bump into possible prey. When they find their target, they sprint and pounce, pinning their prize with their powerful claws. Their name comes from their fondness for stealing honey from bees, but they can eat almost anything, munching on eggs, insects, mice, frogs, snakes and birds.

How to stay safe

↑ **KEEP YOUR DISTANCE.** Honey badgers are most dangerous when they are surprised by something nearby.

✚ **GIVE THEM AN EXIT.** Never corner a honey badger. It will have no option but to fight its way out.

✓ **TALK TO YOURSELF.** If a honey badger hears you coming, then it won't be surprised to see you.

✱ **LEAVE THEM TO IT.** Honey badgers are protective of their young, partners and food, and can get aggressive if these are threatened.

● **BEWARE THE SWEET TOOTH.** Honey badgers are known for their love of honey and often break into people's beehives. If you keep bees, make sure they're very well-protected.

ESCAPE ARTISTS

Honey badgers are very clever. In zoos, they've been known to break out of enclosures by stacking stones and even unlocking doors.

STATUS

Least concern
☐ ☐ ☐ ☐ ☐

Honey badgers are really widespread. With such great self-defence skills and their ability to eat a wide variety of prey, they are able to cope in a changing world.

Tick

| Grassland
◇ Invertebrate

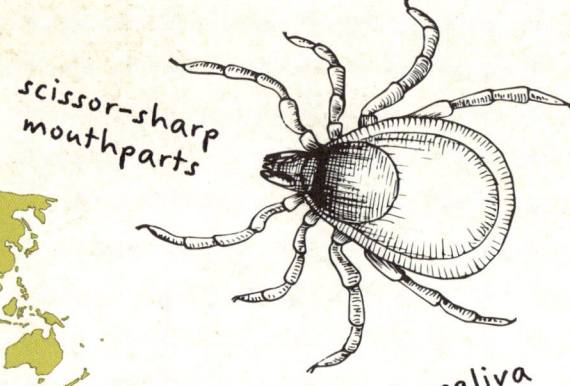

scissor-sharp mouthparts

sticky saliva

Is there anything more 'ick' than a tick on a stick? These eight-legged, bloodsucking beasts are in the same family as spiders and scorpions, but they're even more sneaky. There are thousands of different kinds of ticks. They can be as small as a full-stop and, thanks to their painless bite, victims often don't realise that they've got an unwanted passenger until days after the tick has climbed on. Some animals, such as lions and elephants, end up covered in hundreds of ticks. Some ticks will suck so much blood that they swell to the size of a grape!

Despite their vampire-like diet, most aren't dangerous, but they are a problem because of the horrible diseases they can spread through their saliva. These can cause fevers, pain, and sometimes even death.

Method of attack

Ticks stand on the ends of grass blades, flowers or branches, waiting for an animal to come by. They don't have eyes, but they can sense body heat, shadows and even the breath of a nearby animal. When it comes close, they grab on. They climb to a good area to find blood, where the skin is thin. With mouthparts like scissors, they snip the skin, and push in a drinking tube covered in barbed hooks, making them very hard to remove. Some ticks even make their own version of cement in their saliva to really glue themselves on.

STRANGE SYMPTOMS

Tick bites can cause some odd effects. The lone star tick can make you allergic to meat!

How to stay safe

* **DODGE THE WEEDS.** Try to avoid overgrown areas, where grass and scrub brush against your legs.

✓ **COVER UP.** Wear long trousers and shirts, and tuck your trousers into your socks to cover up your skin.

● **DRESS BOLDLY.** Wear bright clothing, so it's easier to spot ticks climbing on you.

+ **USE BUG SPRAY.** Spray can kill ticks or put them off their dinner.

✗ **AVOID DEER.** Ticks love deer, so don't walk in the areas where there are lots of deer.

● **KEEP AN EYE ON A BITE.** Most tick bites won't give you a disease, but go to a doctor if you feel unwell, especially if the bite has a red ring around it like a bullseye.

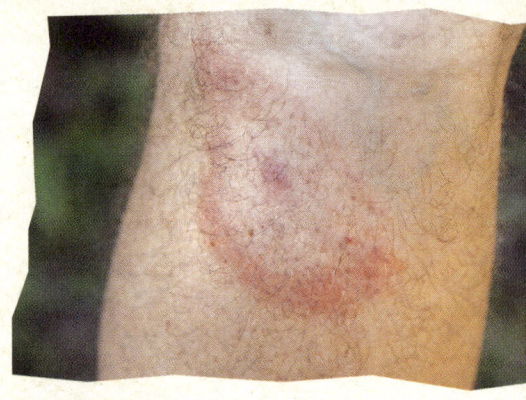

✗ **REMOVE IT.** Ticks need to be removed using a tick remover tool, which looks like a pair of tweezers. They need to be removed as close to the mouthparts as possible.

STATUS

Unknown ☐?☐?☐

There are so many ticks, and they're so tiny, that it's difficult to know their exact numbers. In our increasingly warm and wet world, some ticks are spreading out and being found in places they couldn't be found before.

Ostrich

|||| Grassland

◯ Bird

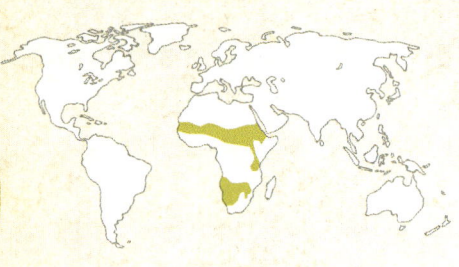

excellent eyesight

spiky claws!

Ostriches are the largest birds in the world. Males can stretch to 2.7 metres tall, almost as high as a basketball hoop, and weigh up to 160 kilograms – as heavy as a sumo wrestler! It's obvious why they can't fly, but that means they need some good defences. Each of their massive feet has just two toes, one of which has a long, dagger-like claw, capable of killing a lion. An ostrich's eyes are larger than its brain, helping them to spot danger from a long way off. Their long legs can run at 64 kilometres per hour, faster than any other bird.

Method of attack

Ostriches can be aggressive when they feel in danger. Males will 'boom', which sounds a lot like a lion's roar. If that doesn't put you off, an ostrich may run right up to you, flapping its wings and raising its head before trying to deliver its deadly kicks.

FUNNY FOOD

Ostriches don't have teeth. They swallow stones and sand to help break up their food.

How to stay safe

- ↑ **KEEP YOUR DISTANCE.** Stay at least 100 metres away from an ostrich to give them plenty of space.

- ● **WATCH OUT FOR PARENTS.** Don't approach parents with eggs or chicks; both male and female ostriches will protect them fiercely.

- ✓ **RUN IF SAFETY IS NEARBY.** They'll kick you in the back if they catch up with you, so only run if you're sure you'll make it.

- ✚ **STAND TO THE SIDE.** Ostriches can only kick forwards, so keep moving round to their side to avoid those claws.

- ↓ **HIDE!** If you can get behind a bush or under cover, they'll soon forget about you.

- ✗ **PLAY DEAD.** If there's no escape, lie face down with your hands over your head. This protects all your soft, squishy parts. The ostrich isn't trying to eat you, so it should lose interest in you after a while.

STATUS

Least concern ▪▪▪▫▫

Ostriches used to live all over Africa and even in parts of Asia, too. Humans hunted them for meat and their feathers, and almost wiped them out. Now ostriches are farmed, so there's less pressure on wild ostriches, and they've been successfully reintroduced to Southern Africa.

Water

Water is where all life began billions of years ago, but it's not our natural home. It's an alien world filled with stings, tentacles, teeth and even electric shocks! With creatures so different to us, it can be hard to understand the danger until it's too late...

Alligator Snapping Turtle

💧 Water

/// Reptile

deadly bite!

sharp claws

Dinosaurs have been extinct for millions of years, but when you stare into the eyes of an alligator snapping turtle, you might wonder if some survived! They can weigh as much as a man, and have sharp claws, a powerful bite and a bad attitude. Masters of disguise, they hide under leaves, piles of sticks and anything else in the water. Even their eyes are camouflaged! Their spiny shells make them look like alligators, which is how they got their name, giving protection in the swamps and rivers of North America. They stay so still for so long that plants and algae grow on them. They have a wide, powerful head and a sharp, deadly beak – strong enough to bite through a broom handle.

Method of attack

Alligator snapping turtles are masterful, sit-and-wait predators. They lie in the water with their lethal, powerful jaws stretched wide. The only thing that moves is their tongue, which looks like a wiggly, pink worm. As little fish approach, they see the 'worm' but not the monster it's attached to. They swim closer, and SNAP! It's all over.

How to stay safe

- **WATCH YOUR WIGGLERS.** Keep fingers, toes and basically anything you want to keep, away from their mouths!

- **WEAR PROTECTION.** Wear thick boots when walking through swamps and rivers in alligator-snapping-turtle territory.

- **KEEP YOUR DISTANCE.** Alligator snapping turtles are often grumpy and can attack to tell you to back off.

- **MIND THE CLAWS.** It's not just their snap you need to watch out for – their claws are sharp enough to leave some nasty scratches.

- **KNOW HOW TO HOLD IT.** If you need to move it (and I don't know why you would!), grab it on the shell behind its head. Alligator snapping turtles can't bite backwards.

STATUS

Vulnerable ■■■□□

Like many creatures that live in water, times are tough for these old survivors. Humans build dams on rivers, take water for crops, and pollute their waterways.

Great White Shark

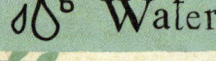
- 💧 Water
- ♥ Fish

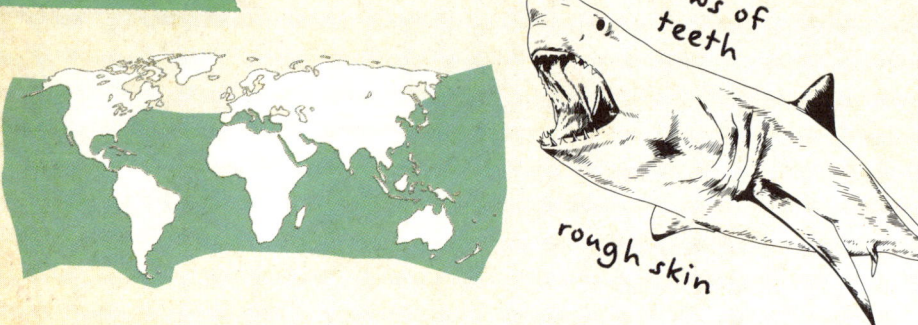

rows of teeth

rough skin

Great white sharks are among the most feared animals in the world, and for good reason. They can grow to over six metres long – about the length of two cars – and weigh as much as a large truck. Their torpedo-shaped bodies can reach speeds of up to 40 kilometres per hour, before they bite down on their target with 300 sharp teeth. Even their skin is so rough and sharp that you could cut yourself just by rubbing against one.

Method of attack

Great white sharks specialise in hunting seals and sea lions. They normally attack from below, lining up their prey at the surface before rocketing up to them. They often attack near dawn and dusk, when the low sun in the sky makes it hard for their prey to see them coming. Their big triangular teeth have serrated edges like a saw, which can cut through bone. Whilst humans aren't their normal prey, great whites have a nasty habit of taking test bites to figure out what we are. Being so large, even an exploratory nibble is sometimes deadly.

SUPER SWIMMERS

Great white sharks can swim huge distances. One swam from South Africa to Australia and back again in just nine months — that's over 19,000 kilometres!

How to stay alive

✗ **DO NOT SPLASH.** Splashing can look like the movements of injured prey, which might make sharks attack.

✓ **STICK TOGETHER.** If you're with other people, position yourselves back-to-back in the water so you can keep an eye on the shark from all angles.

✗ **AVOID DAWN AND DUSK.** Don't swim at sunrise or sunset, as this is the great white shark's favourite time to hunt.

◎ **GET AWAY FROM THE SURFACE.** Shark's often launch at prey on the surface, so it's not the best place for you to be. If you can, get out of the water. If you're scuba diving and that's not an option,stay under the water. Here you can keep a better eye on the shark so it can't sneak up on you, and it will get a better look at you and realise you're not its normal food.

✚ **SUIT UP.** People who dive with sharks regularly wear chainmail suits, like knights in armour.

✗ **AVOID LOOKING LIKE FOOD.** The silhouette of a surfer on a small surfboard looks very like a seal. Hang vertically in the water or stretch your arms and legs out like a starfish.

✗ **AVOID BRIGHT CLOTHING.** Sharks are attracted to bright colours, so avoid wearing bright clothing or shiny jewellery.

! **DEFEND YOURSELF.** If the worst happens and a shark attacks you, punch it with your fist, or something hard like a camera. Aim for the eyes and gills, which are very sensitive, and avoid the teeth!

STATUS

Vulnerable ▣▣▣☐☐

Despite their fearsome reputation, sharks only kill a small number of people each year, while 80 million sharks are killed each year by humans. Their fins are used in shark fin soup which is eaten in some parts of the world.

Stonefish

- Water
- Fish

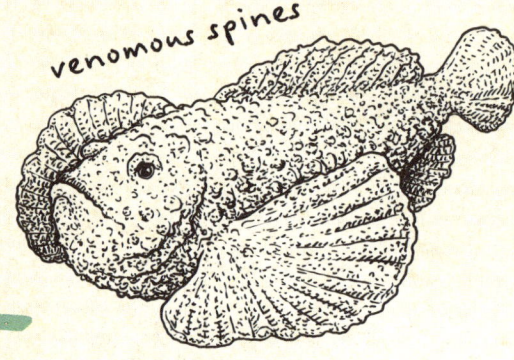

venomous spines

sandy camouflage

Some dangers can be hard to spot. A strange group of fish can be found in tropical oceans around the world. They rest on the bottom of the sea, barely moving, looking more like a lump of rock or coral: the well-named stonefish. Coming in all sorts of shapes and colours, they move so slowly that algae can grow on them. They're not especially big – usually somewhere between a tennis ball and a football. By now you might be thinking, 'How on earth can they be dangerous?'

Well, if you decide to just sit there all day, you'd better have a good defence to protect yourself from predators. Hidden in their dorsal fin (that's the one on top of their body) are a bunch of spines packed with venom. It's the most dangerous venom of any fish and can be deadly to people.

Method of attack

You might think stonefish use that punchy venom to hunt, but no. Instead, this motionless lump of a fish is one of the fastest eaters on the planet. When a small fish comes past, they open their enormous mouth so fast that they suck in anything nearby, all in 0.015 seconds. That's ten times faster than the blink of an eye! Their venomous spines are just used for defence to stop anything bigger swallowing them or, in our case, stepping on them.

How to stay alive

- **WATCH YOUR STEP.** If you're snorkelling, you might be able to see where to safely put your feet, but stonefish camouflage is excellent so take a good look. Not always easy in the surf.

- **WEAR THICK BOOTIES.** Wear wetsuit boots with solid rubber bottoms. They should be strong enough to prevent a stonefish sting. This is always worth doing if you're walking in shallow seas, where corals, urchins and anemones are also a danger.

- **SHUFFLE.** Remember, a stonefish's spines are on the top of its back. If you're not stepping down onto it, but shuffling your feet along the bottom, then you should just encourage it to move out of the way. This isn't foolproof, as they can point their spines in your direction, but the chances of being stung badly are much lower.

- **HAVE HOT WATER NEARBY.** If the worst happens and you get stung, get out of the water as quickly as you can. Chances are that you'll be stung on the hand or foot, so as fast as you can, put it in a bucket and fill it with water as hot as you can stand (but not so hot that it scalds you or blisters). The heat should stop the venom from working and reduce the pain.

STATUS

Least concern

Stonefish don't face many threats. For obvious reasons, they're not popular to handle — and, as they live in shallow rocky areas, they're hard to catch with a net. These strange little wonders are doing just fine.

Great Barracuda

- Water
- Fish

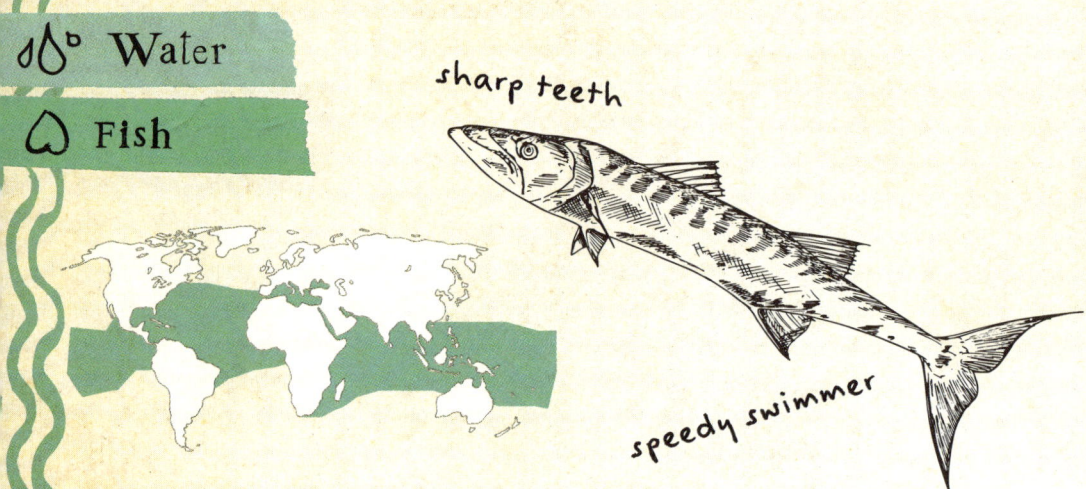
sharp teeth
speedy swimmer

Great barracuda are supreme fish killers. Their powerful tail fin, long thin body and a head sloping to a point allow them to zoom through tropical oceans like a bullet, reaching speeds of over 50 kilometres per hour. They can grow up to two metres long and weigh up to 40 kilograms – as heavy as a large dog. Their long frowning face hides two rows of teeth. The first is on the outside of the jaw, containing hundreds of little razor-sharp teeth. On the inside of the mouth, the second row has much larger dagger-like teeth.

Method of attack

Great barracuda rely on their speed to tackle their prey. They line up a target and charge straight towards it. Smaller fish are swallowed whole, while larger fish are bitten and shaken into smaller chunks. It's very rare, but great barracuda have been known to attack and even kill people. We are definitely not their usual food, so it's likely they might have mistaken a body part or jewellery for a fish.

How to stay safe

✗ **DON'T BE FISHY.** Take off any jewellery or clothing that glitters or looks silvery, which the barracuda might mistake for a fish.

✓ **WEAR GLOVES.** Whether you're on a fishing boat or swimming in the sea, gloves will keep you warm, and protect your hands and fingers if you get closer to a barracuda than you'd like to.

STATUS

Least concern

Although sometimes caught for food, barracuda don't taste particularly nice and can carry diseases. Fortunately, that means they don't have any major threats and are doing well.

Box Jellyfish

◊° Water

◇ Invertebrate

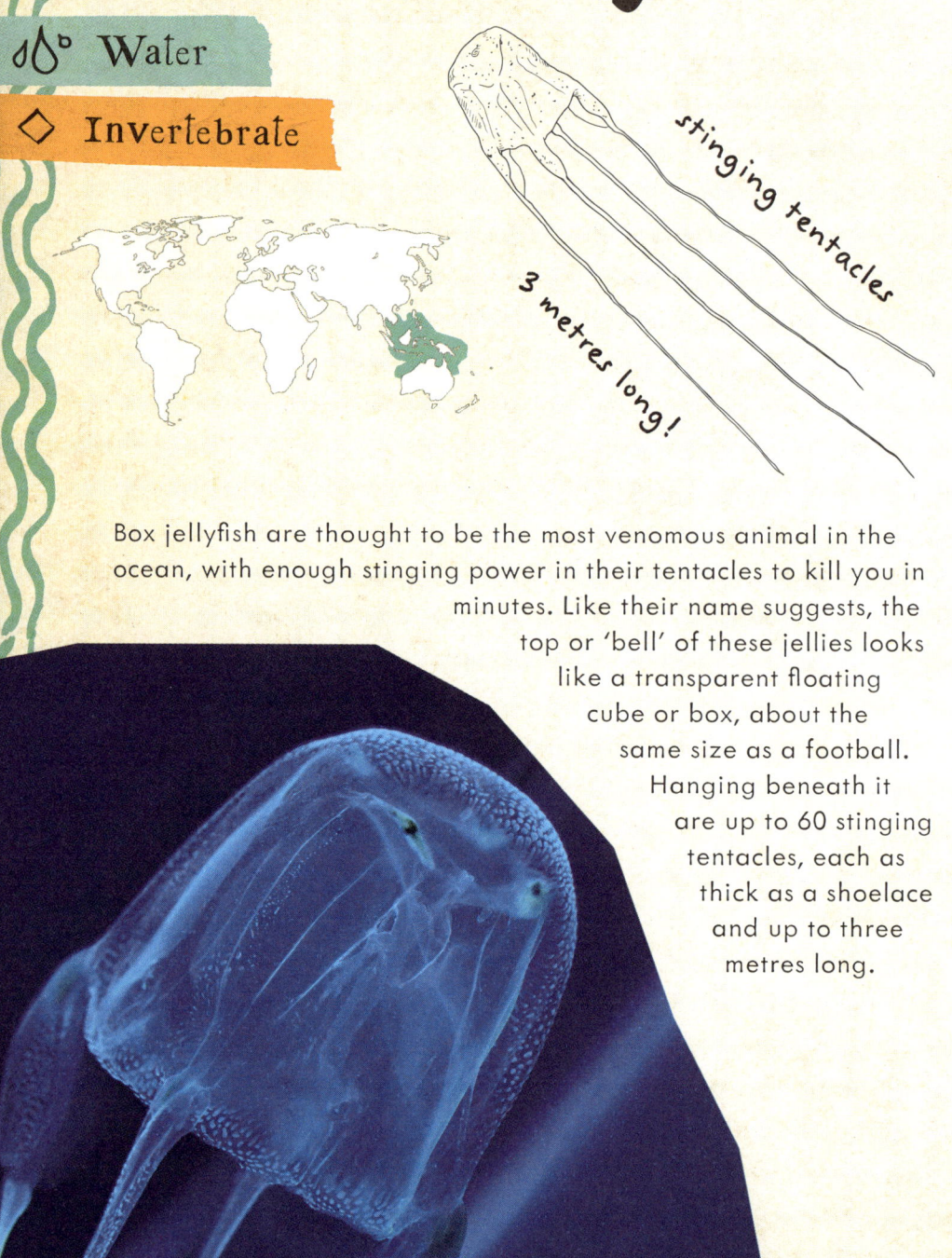

stinging tentacles

3 metres long!

Box jellyfish are thought to be the most venomous animal in the ocean, with enough stinging power in their tentacles to kill you in minutes. Like their name suggests, the top or 'bell' of these jellies looks like a transparent floating cube or box, about the same size as a football. Hanging beneath it are up to 60 stinging tentacles, each as thick as a shoelace and up to three metres long.

Method of attack

Unusually for jellyfish, which normally drift around going where the currents take them, box jellyfish are swimmers. They can swim at roughly our walking speed to move around and hunt down prey. On each of those thick tentacles are millions of tiny, coiled harpoons, waiting to fire into whatever they touch, injecting it with venom. Their preferred food is small fish and shrimp but sadly for us, jellyfish aren't able to stop their tentacles from stinging. Even though we're not on their menu, if we touch their tentacles we'll also get stung.

TIRED TENTACLES

Box jellyfish can become exhausted from all that swimming around. They rest on the seafloor when they're not hunting.

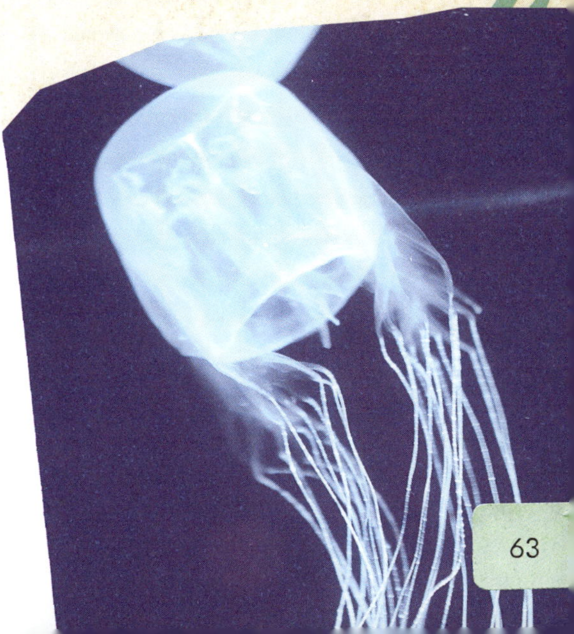

How to stay alive

✓ **SWIM WITH OTHER PEOPLE.** More eyes mean more lookouts. If you see jellyfish (and certainly box jellyfish), it's time to get out of the water.

 COVER YOUR SKIN. If you're swimming in areas known to have lots of jellies, wear a full-body wetsuit complete with booties, gloves and a hood. Jellyfish stings might be powerful, but they're also very small and won't make it through a wetsuit.

 FIGHT JELLY WITH JELLY. Smearing petroleum jelly on your lips and face is another way to protect your skin and can stop a sting.

 STAY CLOSE TO SHORE OR A BOAT. If you see a box jellyfish, you're going to want a quick exit route.

 RINSE THE STING AND GET HELP. If you get stung and you think it was a box jellyfish, call an ambulance, or ask someone to call one for you – box jellyfish mean business. Flush away any tentacles on you. Don't use your hands or they'll get stung too. It can be helpful to use vinegar to soak the stung area for 30 seconds, or just sea water if there's no vinegar nearby. A cold pack or ice in a dry bag can also help with the pain.

STATUS

Unknown ☐ ? ☐ ? ☐

Box jellyfish numbers are very hard to keep track of. It's thought numbers are increasing — which is true for most jellyfish. As our oceans warm up through climate change, jellyfish are one of the few creatures that love those conditions. As one scientist put it, we could be heading for ocean jellification!

Jumbo Squid

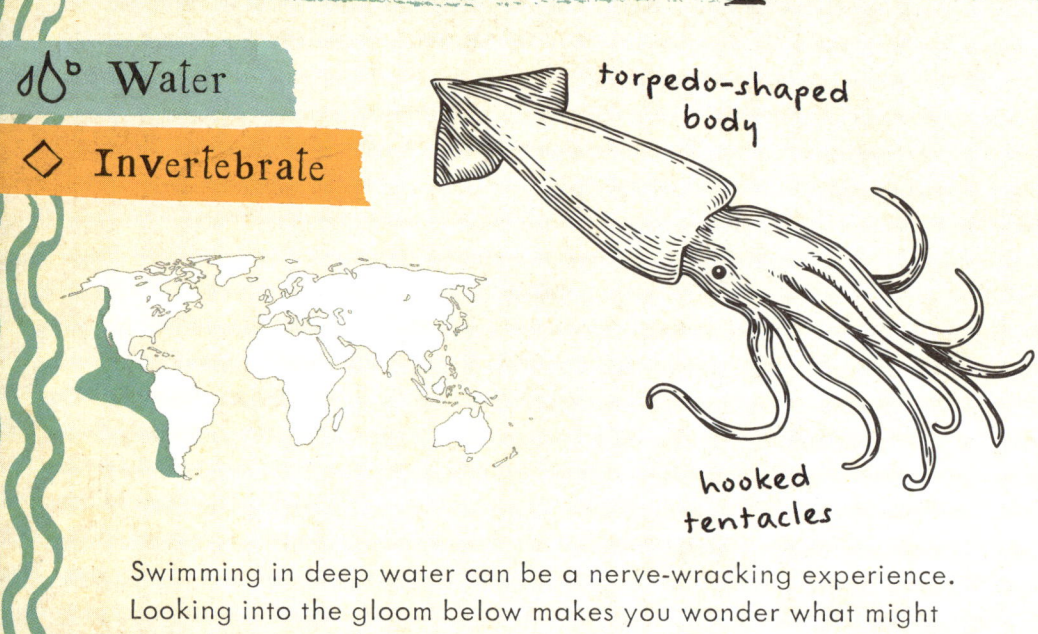

- Water
- Invertebrate

torpedo-shaped body

hooked tentacles

Swimming in deep water can be a nerve-wracking experience. Looking into the gloom below makes you wonder what might be hiding down there. Every night in the tropical waters of the Pacific Ocean that question is answered when millions of jumbo squid come up to the surface to hunt.

At two metres long, and weighing as much as a wolf, their muscular bodies are like mini torpedoes. When they're swimming fast, they keep their eight arms and two long grabbing tentacles pointing tightly forwards. This streamlined shape means they can speed through the water at 24 kilometres per hour – three times faster than an Olympic swimmer!

Method of attack

When they get close to their fishy prey, they open up their tentacles to reveal hundreds of suckers, each covered in sharp little hooks. Once they've grabbed hold of their prey, they pull it towards their slashing beak at the centre of all those arms, which chops it into bits. They can be very aggressive and have been known to attack people with their sucker hooks and biting beak, which is strong enough to chop off fingers.

RED DEVILS

To talk to each other jumbo squid can quickly change colour from white to red and back again. They flash bright red to warn off predators, which is why the fishermen call them 'the red devils'!

How to stay safe

✗ **STAY OUT OF THE WATER.** The easiest way to avoid being attacked by a jumbo squid is to stay out of the water at night. They are sometimes known as 'flying squid' as they can also jump out of the water – so it might be worth avoiding the edge of boats too!

+ **IF YOU DO GO IN, ALWAYS SWIM WITH A BUDDY.** This is a good rule any time you get in the water, but having someone nearby to watch your back and help you out of the water is very important.

✗ **DON'T TURN ON THE LIGHTS.** One of their favourite types of prey is lanternfish, which glow in the dark. If they mistake your lights for lanternfish, you might find yourself being bitten.

✓ **WEAR ARMOUR.** Wear a thick wetsuit or even a metal chainmail suit – like the kind that medieval knights wore to block swords and arrows. They can work to stop sharp squid beaks too.

✗ **BLOCK THAT BEAK.** If you have a camera, a fin, or really anything that's not attached to you, put it between you and the squid. If they bite something hard, they'll soon realise you're not worth it.

STATUS

Unknown ☐ ? ☐ ? ☐

The trouble with spending much of their lives deep underwater is that nobody can be sure how many jumbo squid there are. What we do know is that humans eat a lot of them, and we're catching more of them than ever before — millions each year. Only time will tell if we're catching too many for them to survive.

Banded Sea Krait

💧 Water

/// Reptile

very venomous!

paddle tail

When you think of a venomous snake, the last place you might imagine it hunting is underwater. The banded (also known as yellow-lipped) sea krait is a sea-swimming specialist, able to hold its breath for up to 30 minutes. It dives down from the surface straight towards coral reefs and rocky bottoms, searching in every nook and cranny for other long, thin creatures like eels, their favourite food.

Eels can be dangerous themselves with their strong bodies and sharp teeth, so the banded sea krait must kill them quickly – easily done, as it has one of the most powerful venoms of any snake. To protect itself from other predators like sharks, the snake has a neat disguise: a paddle-like tail shaped a bit like its head, which can be moved around while it's hunting, as if searching for food itself. Predators nearby don't know which is the dangerous 'bitey' end and leave it alone.

Method of attack

Banded sea kraits are generally shy and chilled out (if you're not an eel), so bites are rare. The most likely time to be bitten is if you accidentally catch one in a fishing net and it's already stressed out. Its bite can be deadly.

How to stay alive

✓ **KNOW YOUR SNAKES.**
It's always safest to assume that a snake is venomous, but if you see black-and-white rings on a snake at sea, then definitely keep your distance.

● **WATCH YOUR HANDS.**
Sea snakes stay on the move as they hunt around the reef. If you're snorkelling or diving, be careful placing your hands under rocky ledges, or if you're swimming near holes, in case they pop out.

↓ **LOOK OUT BELOW.**
Sea snakes regularly return to the surface to breathe. If you're swimming above them, remember they'll have to come your way. (I once had a banded sea krait swim up between my legs – I wouldn't recommend the experience!)

 CAREFUL ON DRY LAND.
Banded sea kraits spend half their time on land, sleeping near the shoreline. For much of the day, they rest in rocky crevices or tree hollows, sleeping together in large groups. They're not especially aggressive, but best not to wake them.

 MIND YOUR CATCH.
If you're fishing in banded sea krait territory, then be careful as you haul in your nets or bags. Snakes can be attracted to struggling fish, and if they find themselves caught up, they'll start panicking, leading to them lashing out.

✚ **STAY CLOSE TO A HOSPITAL.**
The only recent death from a banded sea krait happened when the victim was many hours from a hospital. Getting antivenom (a medicine that treats the effects of venom) quickly could save your life.

Least concern 🟩🟩🟩🟩🟩

The good news for banded sea kraits is that they haven't proved to be popular targets for fisher folk, for obvious reasons. Their underwater feeding grounds are sometimes wrecked by dragging trawler nets, heavy anchors or new buildings, but mostly banded sea kraits are doing okay.

Peacock Mantis Shrimp

💧 Water

◇ Invertebrate

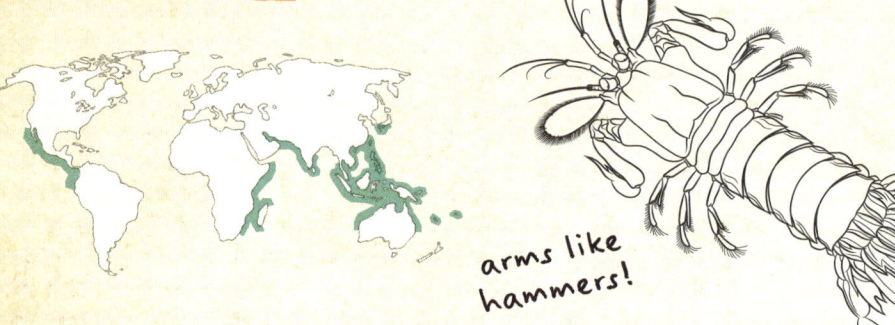

arms like hammers!

I know what you're thinking: 'A shrimp?! How is a shrimp dangerous?' Well, you've clearly never come face to face with a peacock mantis shrimp. They're only the length of a pencil, but these tiddlers are some of the hardest punchers in the animal kingdom, with arms built like hammers. Peacock mantis shrimp have amazing colours. They are so pretty that they often end up in zoos, where zookeepers sometimes give them another name: the thumb splitter!

Method of attack

When the peacock mantis shrimp is on the hunt, it rockets along the seafloor looking for crabs, clams and snails. When it finds them, it stands tall and cocks its arms back, as if stretching an elastic band. When it's ready, it fires its clubbed arms forward, hard enough to bust open shells, knock arms off crabs and – yes – split open thumbs.

EYE SPY

Mantis shrimp have incredible eyes. They can see all kinds of colours and patterns that are invisible to us.

How to stay safe

↑ **KEEP YOUR DISTANCE.** Mantis shrimp don't tend to swim through the water, so if you stay off the seafloor, you should be able to watch them just fine.

+ **DON'T HOLD UP A MIRROR.** If a mantis shrimp sees its reflection, it will think it's a rival and go into fight mode. Camera lenses can get smashed by mantis shrimps that don't like what they see.

@ **DON'T TAP ON THE GLASS.** If you see one in an aquarium, do NOT tap on the glass. Mantis shrimp have been known to smash through tanks.

✓ **STAY OUT OF A SHRIMP'S HOUSE.** Don't put your fingers in their holes if you want to keep your fingers and thumbs in one piece.

✗ **DON'T PICK IT UP.** You probably know why by now...

STATUS

Unknown ☐ ? ☐ ? ☐

Though nobody is certain of their exact numbers, mantis shrimp are quite widespread and don't have many major predators, so they are not in danger of extinction.

Electric Eel

💧 Water

♡ Fish

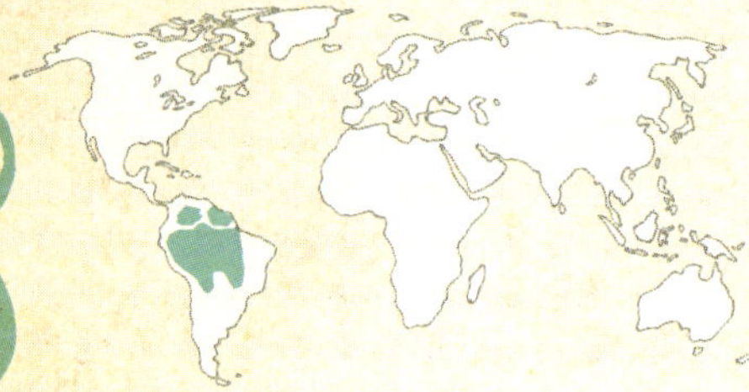

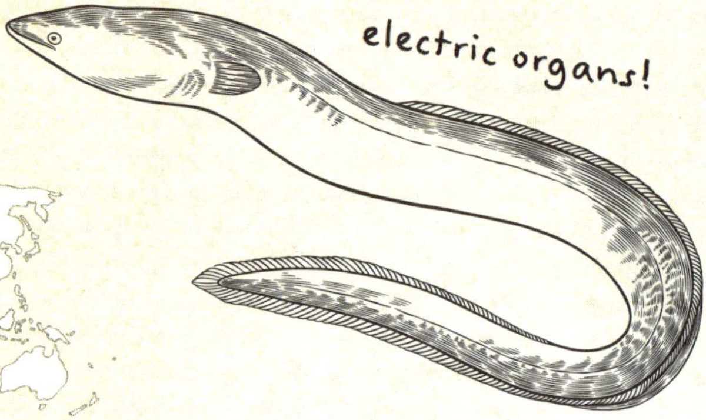

electric organs!

If you were to swim in the rivers of South America, there are many dangers that might give you a surprise, but none as shocking as the electric eel. This fish has an amazing superpower: they can produce over 800 volts of electricity through their skin – that's more than three times as much as the electricity in your home.

Electric eels are very odd fish. Their electricity is so important to them that over three quarters of their body is filled with electricity-making organs, along with other organs like their heart and kidneys. They have to breathe air, and they come up to the surface regularly to do so. They prefer to hunt small fish and mammals at night in deep, murky water, where they're often hard to spot. Electric eels can't see well, but thanks to their special electric body they can sense the animals and area around them, even in complete darkness.

Method of attack

Electric eels use their powerful electric organs for hunting and for defence. They only have small teeth which are rubbish at grabbing onto struggling prey. Instead, they send out a powerful electric shock into the water which stuns anything nearby, making them go limp. Then the electric eel can just suck its prey into its mouth… whole. Like a battery, they can run out of charge after too much action, so they need to rest and recover. Electric eels have been known to stun humans, which causes muscles to stop working and can lead to drowning. They have even been known to stop people's hearts from beating.

THICK SKIN

Electric eels have a protective layer of rubbery, slimy skin to avoid shocking themselves when they unleash their electric blasts.

How to stay alive

✓ **AVOID SWIMMING WITH THEM.** Electricity moves through water very easily, but not through air. If you think electric eels are around, better to stay out of the water.

✗ **DO NOT TOUCH.** An electric eel's power gets stronger the closer you get. If you touch their skin, you're in for a dangerous shock – even if you're on dry land.

🌀 **STAY AWAY FROM THE EDGE.** When frightened, electric eels have been known to jump out of the water, straight onto the threat. By shocking their target through skin contact instead of through the water, they can deliver a much more powerful dose of electricity. They have been seen to stun caiman (a watery beast similar to a crocodile) and even horses this way.

STATUS

Least concern 🟩🟩🟩🟩

Electric eels live in remote areas of South America, and, thanks to their air-breathing habits, they can survive poor-quality water. They have few predators and are rarely eaten by humans. For now, they're doing just fine.

Red-bellied Piranha

💧 Water

🐟 Fish

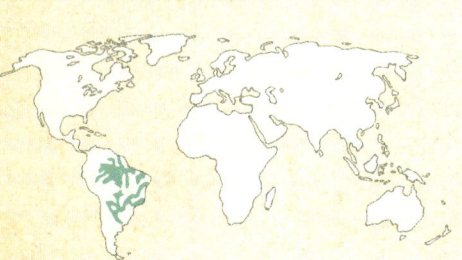

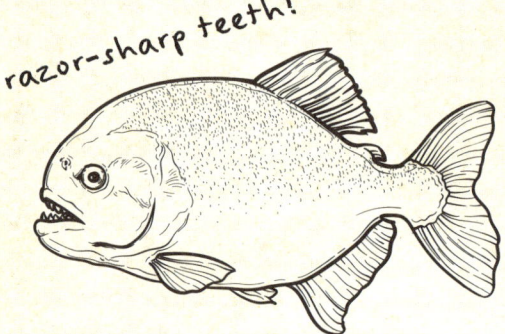

razor-sharp teeth!

In 1914, after a trip to Brazil, American President Theodore Roosevelt wrote about 'the most ferocious fish in the world', worse than sharks or barracuda. He said these frenzied 'man-eaters' could turn a cow into a skeleton in a matter of minutes and would attack anything that entered the water. He was talking about piranhas. Although piranhas can be dangerous, the president didn't get it quite right.

Method of attack

The truth is piranhas are quite shy and fairly calm fish. Many people swim and live alongside them without any problems. They are omnivores and scavengers. They'd prefer a tasty bit of fruit, a plant, a small fish or an easy meal of something already dead, rather than trying to take a chunk out of you. However, their razor-sharp triangular teeth are no joke, and they have been known to attack people if there is no other food around. They can cause serious damage when lots of them start feeding together.

How to stay safe

✗ **AVOID THE DRY SEASON.** If it hasn't rained for a while, rivers and pools where piranhas live can shrink, meaning less chance of food. A desperately hungry piranha is much more likely to try to bite you.

✚ **COVER UP CUTS.** Piranhas live in murky river water where it's hard to see, so they use their other senses to find food. They can sniff out and follow blood in the water.

◎ **STAY CLOSE TO THE BANK.** Swimming in wild rivers can be an amazing experience but stay close to the edge in case you get bitten, and never swim alone.

↑ **FIND A QUICK EXIT.** If you do get bitten, get out as fast as you can. Piranhas often feed as a group and one bite can quickly lead to more.

● **WATCH YOUR CATCH.** Given their appetite, piranhas are easy to catch. When they're flapping around on land, they will bite down on anything, including your fingers.

BARK AND BITE

Piranhas bark to 'talk' to each other or warn off predators.

STATUS

Least concern
☐ ☐ ☐ ☐ ☐

Piranhas are found in good numbers across a large area of South America. Dams blocking their path and pollution filling the rivers are concerns, but their numbers are stable.

Orca

- Water
- Mammal

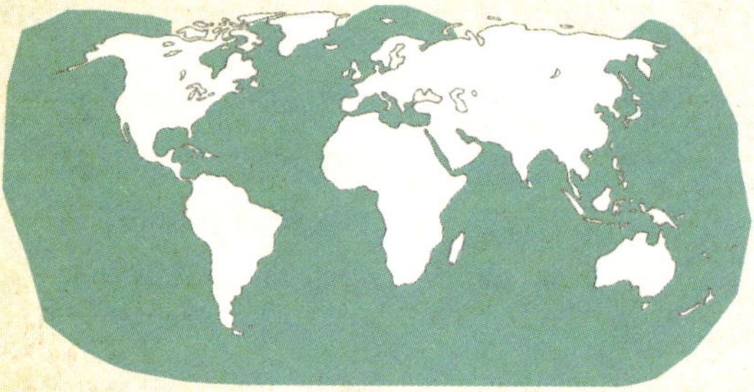

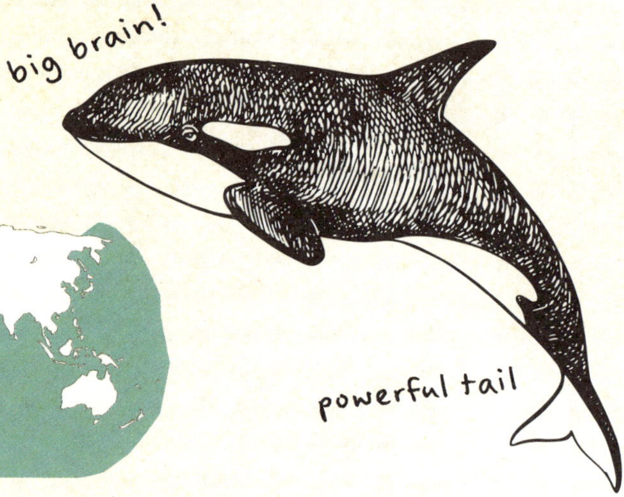

big brain!

powerful tail

Orcas are also known as killer whales, but they aren't actually whales – they are the world's largest dolphins. They are the top predators of the ocean, as they can hunt almost everything, from great white sharks to blue whales. These magnificent creatures can grow to almost ten metres long – about the length of a school bus – and weigh as much as ten tonnes – heavier than a tractor. Orcas live in family groups, or 'pods', of around five to ten animals led by an older, experienced female – the matriarch.

Method of attack

One of the greatest weapons an orca has is its extraordinary brain. They use all sorts of clever tricks to target different prey. They can blow bubbles to confuse and trap fish; use their heavy bodies like a battering ram for large whales; and sometimes a whole pod will swish their tails at the same time to create a big wave to knock seals off ice floes (floating sheets of ice). They have even been seen to karate-chop sharks on the head with their tail fins, before flipping them over onto their backs, which strangely makes the sharks fall asleep and become harmless.

LONG-LIVED HUNTERS

Orcas can live up to 90 years in the wild.

How to stay safe

● **LOOK HUMAN.** Amazingly, there has only ever been one recorded attack on a human in the wild, where an orca bit a surfer's leg before quickly letting go. There were sea lions in the area and it seems the orca confused the surfer for a sea lion. The lesson here is don't *look* like their prey, and don't swim near their prey!

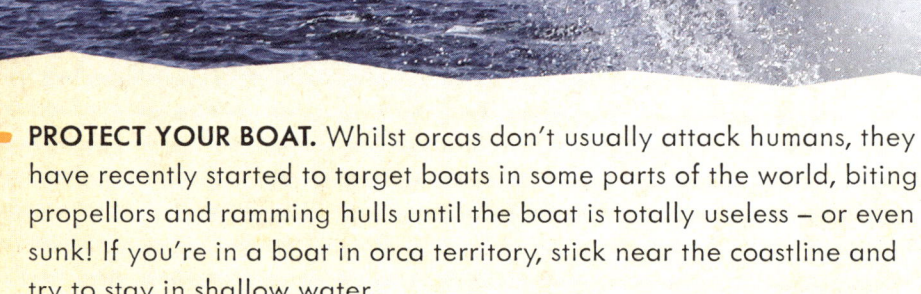

➕ **PROTECT YOUR BOAT.** Whilst orcas don't usually attack humans, they have recently started to target boats in some parts of the world, biting propellors and ramming hulls until the boat is totally useless – or even sunk! If you're in a boat in orca territory, stick near the coastline and try to stay in shallow water.

✓ **KNOW YOUR ORCA.** While some orcas eat mammals, others will only eat fish, making them even less likely to attack us. To tell which is which, scientists and guides take lots of photos. Each orca has its own colour pattern and fin shape, which is as individual as our fingerprints.

✗ **DON'T SUPPORT ORCAS IN CAPTIVITY.** It may be tempting to get a better look at an orca in a theme park or aquarium, but they are much too big and intelligent to live in such a small space. The only times orcas have killed people is in captivity, when they've been under extreme stress.

STATUS

Unknown ☐ ? ☐ ? ☐

It's difficult to know all the challenges that orcas might face for survival. They live far out at sea and can travel huge distances, making it hard to keep track of them or know how many there are. We do know that humans catch huge amounts of the same kind of fish that some orcas eat, so there may not be enough left for them. We also know that old fishing equipment can entangle them.

Desert

Deserts are difficult places to survive. With so little food and water, it's hard for animals to find a meal, and stay off the menu themselves. The creatures here have developed incredible weapons to defend themselves and go on the attack.

Deathstalker Scorpion

- Desert
- Invertebrate

deadly venom
sharp stinger

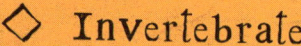

Scorpions are the little problem you don't see coming! Small enough to fit in the palm of your hand, the deathstalker scorpion holds enough venom inside its large yellow stinger to kill. These hardy animals are found in deserts and dry scrubland across North Africa and the Middle East. With a tough exoskeleton (hard outer shell), they're permanently walking around in a suit of armour. Their strong pincers are sharp enough to snip through skin. Like most scorpions, the deathstalker is nocturnal, which means it comes out at night to hunt for prey. During the day it hides away... and that's when it can be most dangerous!

Method of attack

Scorpions use their sting in both attack and defence. So whilst we'd never be on their menu, that doesn't mean we wouldn't be on the receiving end of their deadly venom if they think we're a threat. Deathstalker scorpions are mostly bug hunters, eating crickets, spiders and worms. They have good vision and an excellent sense of smell to help them track down their prey. When prey is in sight, they raise their chunky tail high above their head and bring down the sharp stinger onto their victim in the blink of an eye. The sharp tip is extra strong and can even pierce the tough shell of other scorpions. A fleshy human is no match for the deathstalker!

LIQUID GOLD

Deathstalker venom is the most valuable liquid in the world – doctors use it to treat cancer and other diseases. If you could collect enough to fill a large milk bottle, it would be worth millions!

How to stay alive

↓ **CHECK YOUR SHOES.** A classic place for scorpions to hide during the day are the shoes you left on the ground. Turn them upside down and give them a hard tap to shake out any inhabitants.

↓ **CHECK THE BED.** Just as you're drifting off to sleep, your hand finds something crawling under the pillow... it's the stuff of nightmares!

✓ **KNOW YOUR SCORPIONS.** This is a handy rule: BIG pincers = SMALL venom. SMALL pincers = BIG venom. Try to avoid all scorpions, but stay well away from the ones with small pincers.

SHAKE OUT YOUR CLOTHES AND TOWELS. Before you dress for the day or jump in the shower, give your clothes and towels a thorough shake down to lose any scorpions that might be clinging on.

+ **GET A BLACK LIGHT.** A black light is a type of purple torch that makes certain things glow in the dark. Strangely, scorpions glow very brightly when you shine a black light on them!

✱ **TURN ON THE LIGHTS.** Scorpions hate the light and will quickly scuttle back to the darkness.

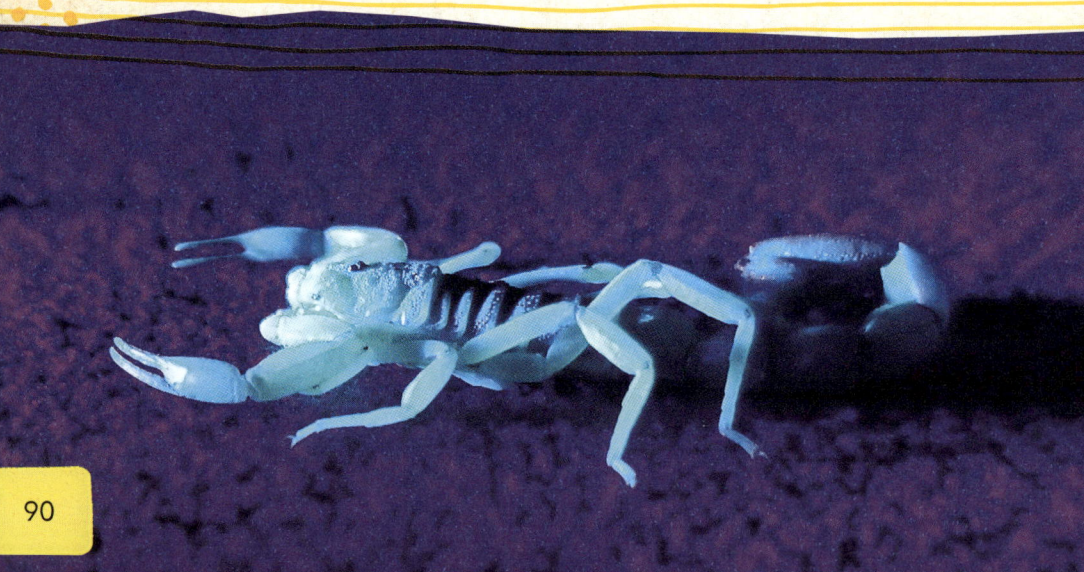

STATUS

Unknown 🔲?🔲?🔲

Minibeasts are small, secretive and often either hard to find or are in such large numbers that they're hard to count. For the deathstalker scorpion we have no idea how many there are. We do know that habitat destruction and collecting them from the wild, for either medical research or to sell as pets, is reducing their numbers.

Six-eyed Sand Spider

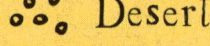
Desert

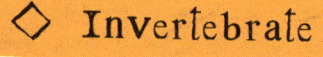
Invertebrate

three pairs of eyes

twig-like legs

Picture a desert so dry that sometimes it doesn't get a single drop of rain all year round and so hot that the temperature of the sand can reach 60° C. This is what life is like in the Namib desert in southern Africa. To make matters worse, it's also home to one of the most venomous spiders on the planet, which hides just beneath the surface, waiting for their next victim to wander past.

Six-eyed sand spiders have a flat, chunky body not much larger than a fingertip, and long legs which they spread out wide. They can move scarily fast when they need to, but much of their life is spent sitting still, trying not to waste energy. Deserts are such a hard place to survive that not many creatures live there. The spiders can be waiting a long time for prey to come past. It's thought they can survive for up to a year without food or water.

Method of attack

Six-eyed sand spiders find a good spot and push their flat bodies low against the desert surface, while their long legs fling sand over their backs and heads to disguise them. With a few last shuffles of their legs to hide themselves, they're practically invisible. Stretched out, they can feel the vibrations of any passing prey such as other spiders, scorpions or geckos. When something wanders into the trap, the spider strikes with lightning speed, delivering a killer dose of venom, strong enough to make sure the spider gets its meal.

How to stay alive

↑ **STAY ON YOUR FEET.** Don't sit, lie or crawl on dunes where spiders might be present. If you do need to sit, check the area carefully with a thick boot or stick first.

✓ **CHECK YOUR CLOTHES.** Spiders love hiding in clothes and shoes, so check before putting them on. Bites normally happen when spiders have been squashed or sat on.

✗ **DON'T SLEEP ON THE GROUND.** Rolling on one of these spiders in the night will give you real-life nightmares.

+ **KNOW THE NEAREST HOSPITAL.** Sometimes it's hard to know which bug bit you, but if you're in six-eyed sand spider territory, it's better to go and get it checked out.

↓ **WATCH OUT FOR 'TWIGS'.** Sometimes you can spot the brown, outstretched legs of waiting spiders poking out of the sand, looking just like little twigs.

Unknown ☐ ? ☐ ? ☐

STATUS

The six-eyed sand spider lives in a hard place to study, and is so secretive and shy that it's difficult to know how many there are. One of the upsides of living in a place where few can survive is that there is little impact from humans, so they're probably doing just fine.

Red Kangaroo

- Desert
- Mammal

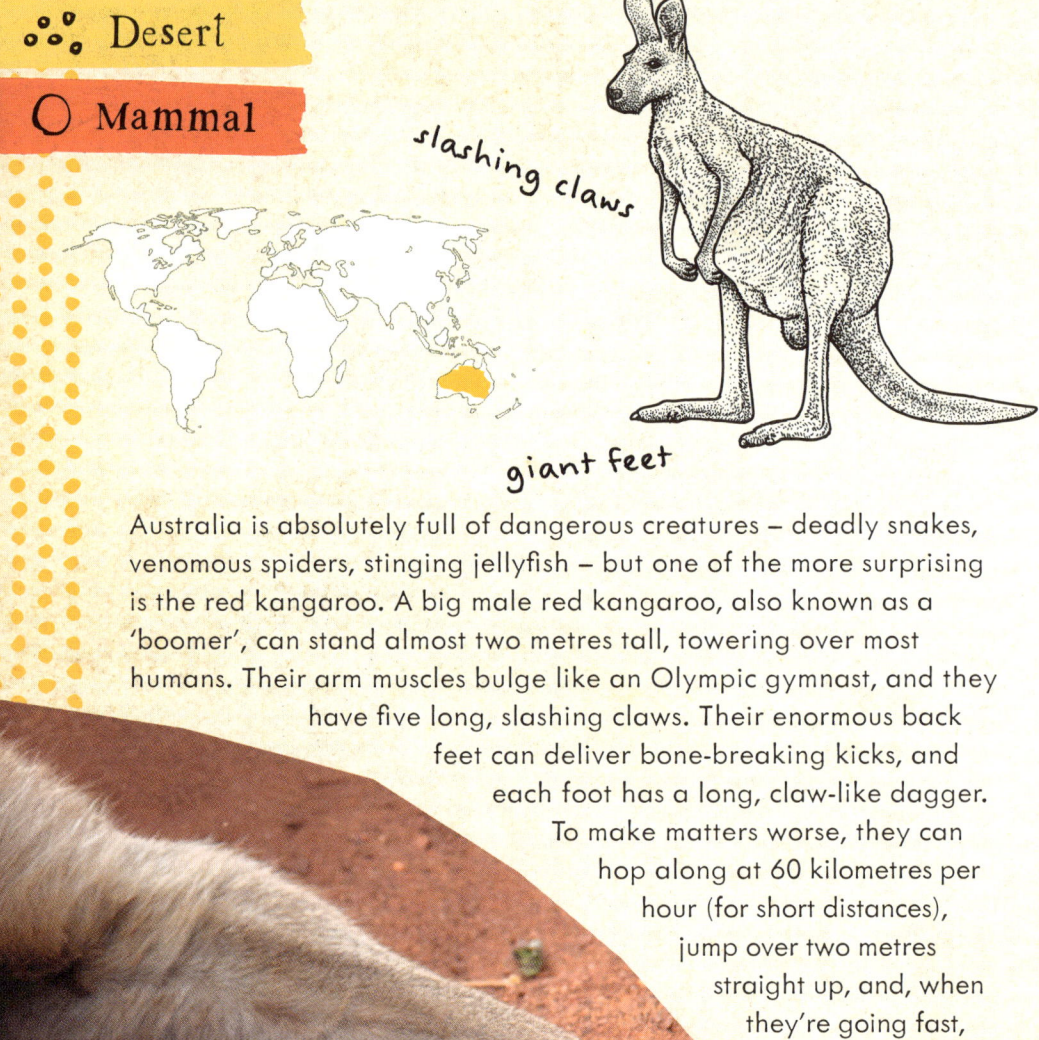

slashing claws

giant feet

Australia is absolutely full of dangerous creatures – deadly snakes, venomous spiders, stinging jellyfish – but one of the more surprising is the red kangaroo. A big male red kangaroo, also known as a 'boomer', can stand almost two metres tall, towering over most humans. Their arm muscles bulge like an Olympic gymnast, and they have five long, slashing claws. Their enormous back feet can deliver bone-breaking kicks, and each foot has a long, claw-like dagger. To make matters worse, they can hop along at 60 kilometres per hour (for short distances), jump over two metres straight up, and, when they're going fast, can easily bound the length of a school bus. In short, you're not going to outrun them.

Life can be hard in the Australian desert. It barely rains, there's not much to eat, and the landscape is so massive that it can be hard to find a mate. No wonder red kangaroos are very protective of whatever food, water, young, and mates they've managed to find. In fact, they could beat you up if they think you're trying to take pretty much anything!

Method of attack

Kangaroos square up to each other like boxers, getting close enough to slash and punch with their arms. They lean back on their thick tail and take both feet off the ground to deliver a double kick!

How to stay safe

↓ **KEEP YOUR DISTANCE.** Kangaroos are a joy to watch from far away – just don't get too close.

✗ **DON'T FEED THEM.** Kangaroos can get angry when they're hungry. If you feed them lots of sugary human food and it runs out, they can lash out!

✱ **LEARN TO SPEAK KANGAROO.** Crouch and let out a low grunt or cough. That's kangaroo talk for admitting defeat. Hopefully they'll accept your surrender and leave you alone!

◉ **GO AROUND THEM.** Red kangaroos are fantastic at hopping, but terrible at walking. Their big feet are quite clumsy when they're at a standstill. Rather than run away from them, try running around them.

+ **FIND A BLOCKER.** Position yourself so something is between the two of you – ideally a big tree.

✓ **GIVE THEM SOMETHING ELSE TO BEAT UP!** Throw something at them, like a hat or a water bottle, for them to attack while you make an exit.

↑ **LEARN THE BODY LANGUAGE.** If a male kangaroo wants to show dominance, it might start pulling up grass, attacking trees, or flexing its muscles. It might look funny, but you're next! Time to make a quick exit.

↓ **DROP AND PLAY DEAD.** If there's really no escape, drop to the floor, curl up into a ball and protect your face and neck with your arms. Remember – a kangaroo isn't trying to eat you! Once it feels it's 'won', it will leave you alone.

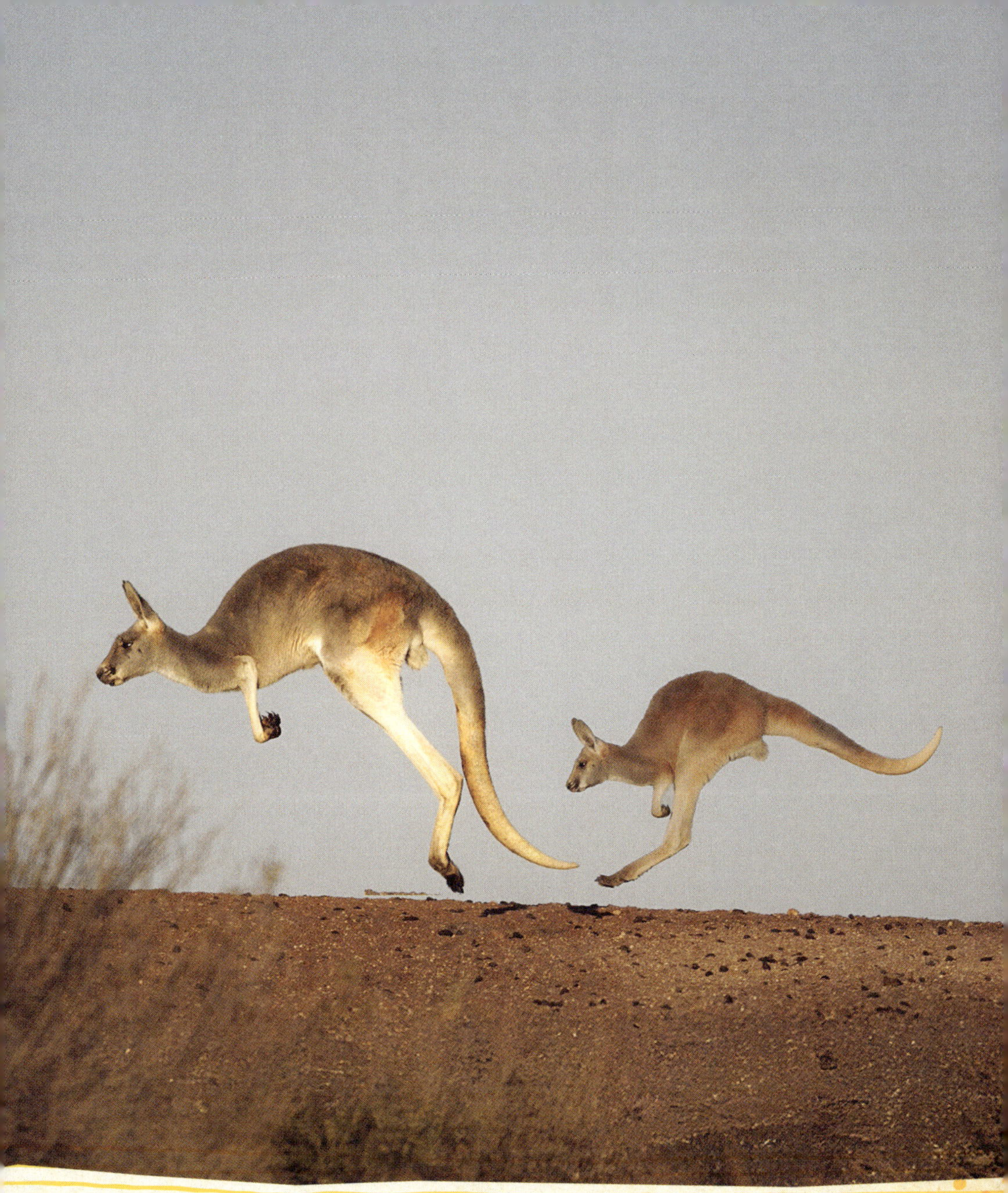

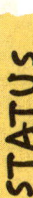

Least concern 🟩🟩🟩🟩

Red kangaroos are born survivors. There are millions of them hopping through the Australian outback!

Inland Taipan

Desert

Reptile

killer bite

very powerful venom!

The inland taipan or 'fierce snake' is poorly named because it is in fact very shy, even though it stretches to over two metres long and has a strong, thick body. It lives in the dry central area of Australia known as 'the outback', where it rarely, if ever, meets a human, and tries to quickly slither away if it does. Its name comes from its venom which is *incredibly* fierce. It's the most powerful venom in the world, a single bite is able to kill about 100 adult humans. Fortunately, the normal targets for its fangs are rats and small marsupials. With a bite packing such a powerful punch, the snake doesn't have to let go of its prey after a strike and can enjoy its dinner straight away.

Method of attack

The fierce snake is diurnal, meaning it is active during the day. After a morning basking in the sun, it seeks out prey in their burrows or in deep cracks in the earth where there is no escape. It strikes very quickly, sometimes more than once, in rapid fire. Bites on humans are defensive bites. Other snakes might 'dry bite' humans as a warning, where they just whack us with their chins or sink their fangs in without releasing any of their venom. It would be a waste using it on something they can't eat. However, the inland taipan is dangerously unusual, in that even its defensive bites are almost always packed with venom.

How to stay alive

✓ **KEEP YOUR HANDS AND FEET WHERE YOU CAN SEE THEM.** Avoid long grass, stepping over logs, or grabbing onto branches when you're in snake country.

✚ **STAMP YOUR FEET AS YOU WALK.** Snakes don't have good hearing, but they can feel vibrations through the earth and will move out of your path.

↓ **LOOK OUT FOR THE S-SHAPED WARNING.** This fierce snake will form a low S-shape when it's threatened, rearing the front part of its body up and backwards while its head stays pointing forwards. It's time to back off!

● **TAKE A PHOTO IF IT IS SAFE TO DO SO.** If you've been bitten, it can be lifesaving to get a picture of the snake that bit you. Snake venom can act in different ways depending on which snake bit you, and each can need a different antivenom — so it's great information for the doctor. Zoom in, so you can keep a safe distance.

✚ **STAY CALM AND GET HELP.** After a snake bite, it's important to move as little as possible and stay calm — as this slows down the heart rate, which slows the spread of venom around the body. An ambulance should be called, and a bandage should be wrapped tightly around, above and below the bite while waiting for help to arrive.

STATUS

Least concern 🟩🟩🟩🟩🟩

The inland taipan is doing just fine. They live in such hard-to-reach places that we don't have much of an impact on them.

Vampire Bat

- Desert
- Mammal

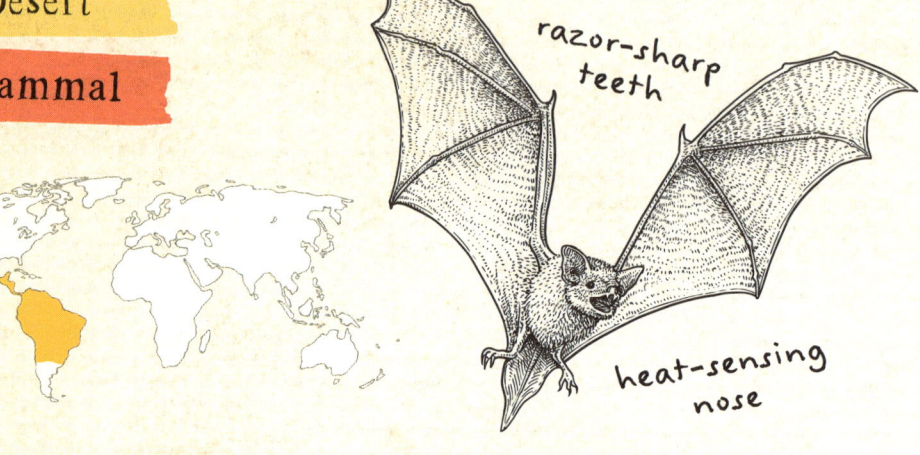

razor-sharp teeth

heat-sensing nose

Vampire bats have a terrifying reputation for flitting through the night, sucking your blood and turning you into a vampire. You'll wake up looking very pale, with a desire to avoid sunlight and holy water. Fortunately, that's just a myth... or is it?

In reality, vampire bats are just like flying mice – they could fit in the palm of your hand, and they're brown and furry. It's their grizzly feeding habits that are less cute: they feed only on blood, which they get from animals like seals and cattle. They only take a small amount, but the real danger is the disease they can carry in their bite – rabies. This horrid virus can kill you, as well as make you sensitive to light, and strangely it can make you utterly frightened of water. Sound familiar?

Method of attack

Vampire bats fly at dusk to look for prey. They have excellent hearing and target animals that are fast asleep and breathing heavily. Their hearing is so good they can pick out the individual snore of the same animal night after night, so they can come back and just unpick the scab from the bite the night before. Special heat sensors on their nose sniff out the best place to find hot blood beneath thin skin. On cows and pigs, that's normally around the head and neck; on humans, it tends to be on fingers and toes. Razor-sharp triangular teeth make a tiny five-millimetre hole and the bats lap up the blood with their tongue. Their saliva contains a powerful painkiller, so the sleeping victim is totally unaware.

SUPER DROOL

Vampire bat saliva has something in it called 'draculin' which keeps the blood flowing. Scientists are investigating how it might be used to help people who have blood clots (little blockages in their blood vessels).

How to stay alive

✗ **DON'T SLEEP OUTDOORS.** Vampire bats usually prey on farm animals and wildlife, so avoid seeming like one of the herd.

↑ **ZIP YOURSELF IN.** If you are going to sleep outdoors, do it inside a tent or mosquito net to keep bats out.

● **TURN ON THE LIGHTS.** Like most bats, vampire bats are nocturnal and hide in the dark. Bright lights should keep them away.

✱ **MAKE SOUNDS.** Vampire bats are super sneaky, preferring to feed on sleeping victims. If you keep the radio on, they may avoid you.

✓ **KEEP ANIMALS INDOORS.** If there's no other food around for the vampire bats, then they might leave the area.

✚ **TAKE MEDICINE.** Rabies is a deadly disease, but vaccinations are available if you think you might catch it.

Least concern ☒☒☒☐☐

STATUS

Vampire bats are widespread and able to adapt to a changing world. Whilst farming can be devastating for some wildlife, for bats that just means more animals to feed on.

Dromedary Camel

- Desert
- Mammal

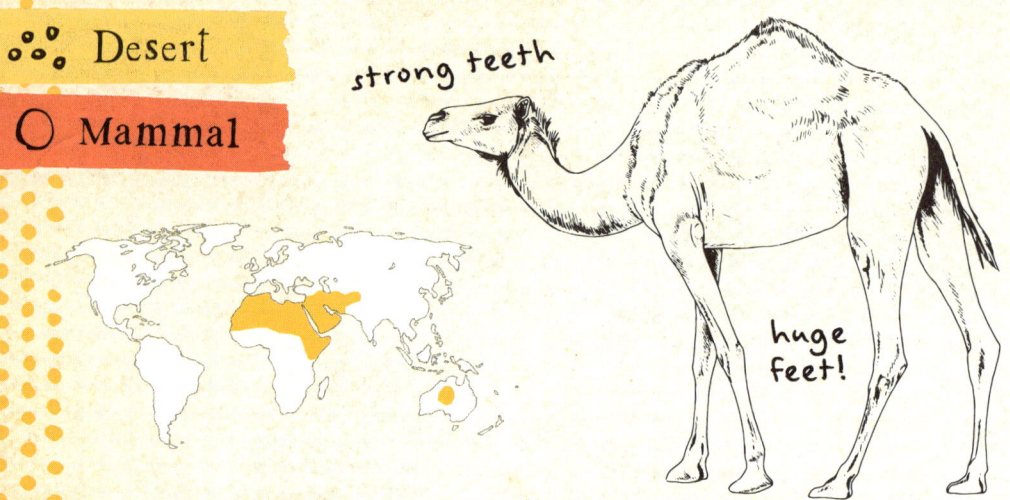

strong teeth

huge feet!

With their fluttering eyelashes and goofy smile, you might not think camels are dangerous – but in parts of the world, like The Gulf, camels cause more than eight out of ten animal-related injuries. Weighing 500 kilograms and standing over two metres high, they tower over most people. They're strong enough to grab you with their teeth, lift you off the ground and hurl you, even lifting animals as heavy as donkeys!

Method of attack

Camels are normally relaxed around humans and most injuries happen by accident from riders falling off or camels stepping on them. However, they can be grumpy and unpredictable. During the breeding season, males can become very aggressive and bites can be more serious, even deadly.

SANDY SUPERPOWERS

Camels have two pairs of eyelashes to keep out sand and they can close their nostrils in a sandstorm.

How to stay safe

- **WATCH FOR THE TONGUE FLAP.** During the breeding season, males inflate a sort of pink balloon out of their mouth, which is called a 'dulla'. It might impress the females, but you should stay back.

- **READ THEIR ENERGY.** Camels that look alert and are holding their head high might be stressed and more likely to attack. If a camel is making a lot of noise, jumping or trembling, it might also be a sign of stress – all signs to keep away.

- **WATCH THOSE TOES.** Camels have huge feet. Their toes spread out so they don't sink in sand, but it's not much fun to be stepped on.

- **BE KIND.** Camels hold a grudge and remember poor treatment. Be gentle and calm, and they should be the same with you.

STATUS

Domesticated

Humans have always found one-humped camels very useful. They provide meat, skin, transport, milk – even their dry poo can be used for making fires. There are millions of dromedary camels around the world, including a large number in Australia living free.

Saw-scaled Viper

- Desert
- Reptile

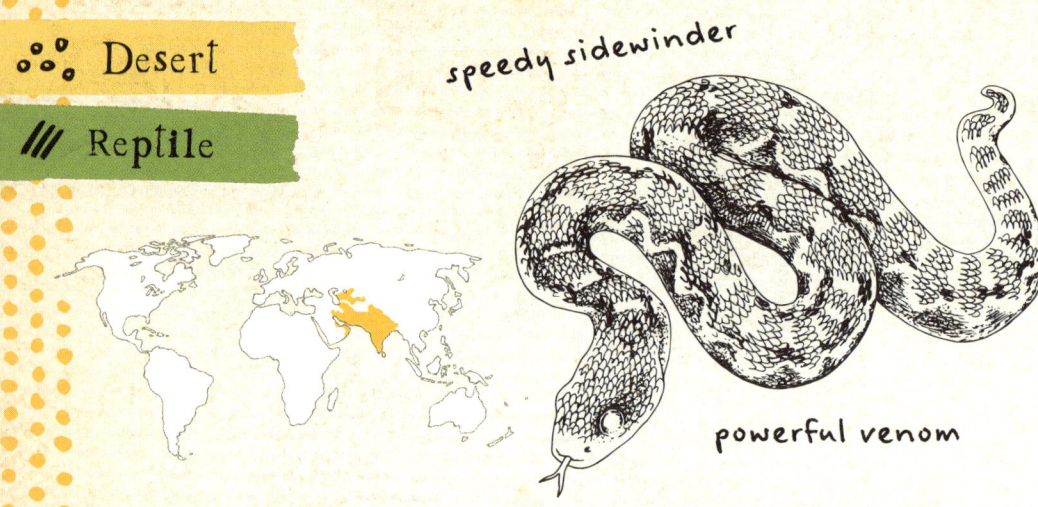

speedy sidewinder

powerful venom

The most dangerous animal is usually not the fastest, the strongest, or the most venomous... it's simply the one you're closest to. The saw-scaled viper kills more people than any other snake in the world, and this is because it lives alongside millions of people in Asia. This pretty, mottled-brown snake is only the width of a sausage and not much longer than your arm, but looks can be deceiving – it's got a temper. These vipers are quick to strike if they feel threatened, and they have a powerful venom. About one in five bites are deadly if the victim doesn't get medicine in time.

Saw-scaled vipers spend most of their day in burrows, cracks in the earth or under rocks, where their colour patterns provide camouflage from predators. They sit in a coiled-up shape, with their head at the centre, ready to strike.

Method of attack

Humans aren't the normal targets for saw-scaled vipers. They mostly hunt from dusk until dawn, looking for bugs and rodents. They are mainly ambush hunters, sitting and waiting for passing prey, but they can move scarily fast when they want to.

WEIRD WIGGLE

Saw-scaled vipers are 'sidewinders'. With their head pointing forwards, their body races along beside them, wiggling sideways.

How to stay alive

✓ **USE YOUR EARS.** When threatened, saw-scaled vipers bunch up in a coil and move their body in a mesmerising dance. As their rough scales grind against each other, they make a buzzing sound.

✗ **DON'T GO BAREFOOT.** Due to their small size, most bites from these vipers are on the foot or lower leg of people who accidentally step on them. Wear thick boots or 'snake gaiters', which act like a bullet-proof vest for your lower legs.

↓ **STOMP YOUR FEET.** You might think tiptoeing around is a safer way to walk, but giving snakes plenty of warning is a good idea as they can feel vibrations through the ground. Just check where your feet are going to land as you stomp.

● **WATCH YOUR HANDS.** A lot of saw-scaled viper bites happen on farmland, where people are using their hands to work the soil. These snakes like to hide under rocks which people might pick up. Their camouflage increases the risk of not being spotted.

+ **GET SOME AMAZING ANTIVENOM.** The one upside of saw-scaled vipers being such regular biters is that doctors have had plenty of practice trying to treat venomous bites. Scientists have created an antivenom that was specially made to fight the effects of saw-scaled viper venom.

STATUS

Least concern 🟩🟩🟩🟩

Understandably, saw-scaled vipers aren't often popular neighbours and people sometimes kill them. However, they're found over such a large area with plenty of hidey-holes, which means these little snakes continue to thrive.

Gila Monster

- Desert
- Reptile

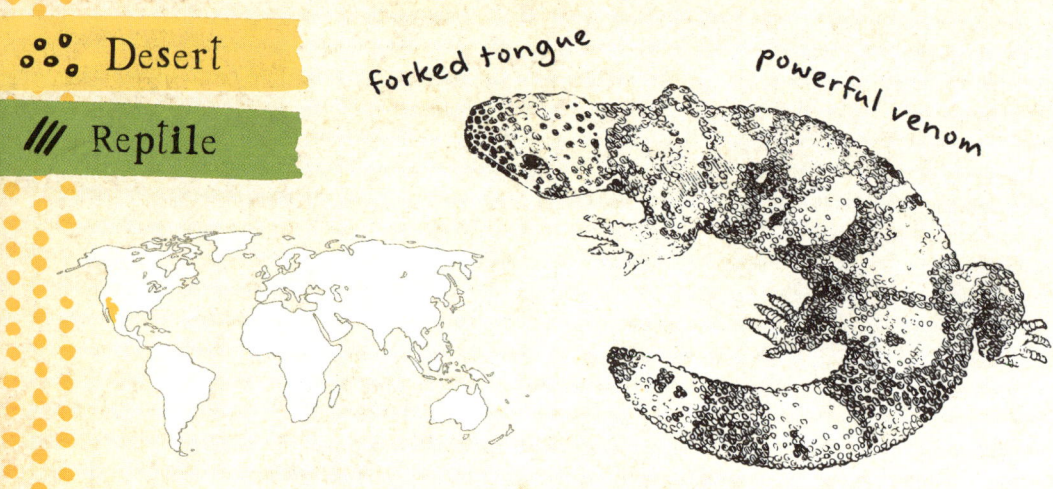

In the baking hot deserts of North America, real-life monsters roam amongst forests of cactus. The gila (pronounced 'healer') monster is a very strange lizard indeed. At 50 centimetres long with a stocky build, it's the largest lizard in North America and one of only a handful of lizards in the world to have a venomous bite. The venom can cause excruciating pain and, in rare cases, death.

Despite their fearsome weapons, they're very pretty. Their scaly skin looks like it's covered in colourful beads. They are mostly black with bands and blotches of yellow, red and pink, which has led people to want to keep them as pets. That's often where the accidents happen. In the wild, gila monsters mostly hunt creatures like rabbits, mice, birds and other lizards, as well as eggs. They can eat up to half their own bodyweight in one sitting – a useful trick if you don't know when your next meal is going to come along.

Method of attack

To find food, gila monsters taste the air with their black forked tongue and use it to follow the scent of their prey. They might look slow but, when they want to, they can strike with ferocious speed and bite down hard. They sometimes flip onto their back mid-bite to try and squeeze more venom out. Although they do have a powerful venom, it's thought that they don't use it often for hunting. Instead, they mostly use this in defence, which is bad news for humans.

RECYCLED URINE

It's so hot and dry in the desert that gila monsters use their bladders like a water bottle, storing lots of water whenever they find it. During a dry spell, they can suck the water from their wee back into their blood.

How to stay alive

- **READ THE WARNING SIGNS.** A grumpy gila monster will flash its jaws open wide towards you, revealing a sinister-looking black mouth.

- **LISTEN UP.** A hissing gila monster is not happy – stay back.

- **SUIT UP.** Wear sturdy ankle-high boots and socks when you're in gila-monster territory. Not only will they protect you from the gila monster's bite, but there are plenty of snakes and cactus needles in those parts too.

- **AVOID HOLES.** Don't put your hands down burrows or into hollow logs. Gila monsters spend most of their life underground, out of the sun, and they won't appreciate intruders.

- **KEEP YOUR DISTANCE.** This is the easiest way to keep everyone safe.

Near-threatened ☐☐☐☐☐

STATUS

Gila monster numbers are sadly falling pretty quickly. Roads and canals stop them getting around safely, and new houses and towns are being built in areas where they live.

Saltwater Crocodile

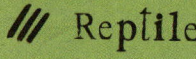
Desert

Reptile

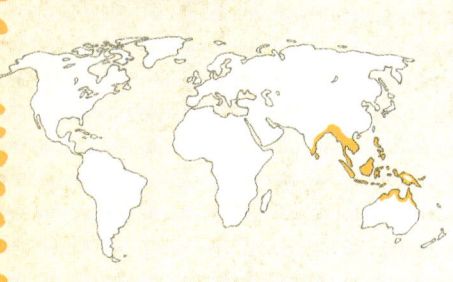

muscular tail

powerful bite

Saltwater crocodiles are the largest reptiles on the planet. Big males can be over six metres long, as long as two cars. They can weigh over 1,000 kilograms – that's as heavy as two polar bears! With over 60 large teeth, they clamp down on their prey with the most powerful bite force recorded for any living animal. Their tough armoured scales are bulked up with bony plates. It's little wonder they have no natural predators.

Saltwater crocodiles are iconic creatures of the dry Australian outback, but they can also be found in the more tropical waters of Southeast Asia. Although they're called saltwater crocs, they can live in both salt and freshwater, though mainly they tend to be found near coastlines.

Method of attack

Saltwater crocs are master ambush hunters. They can go for a year without eating, so they don't mind waiting for the perfect time to strike. They sit at the surface with only their nostrils and eyes poking above the surface, looking just like a floating branch. They mostly hunt at the water's edge, waiting for prey like deer, boar or buffalo – and yes, even humans. With one quick lunge, they snap down onto their target and drag it into the water to drown it. If it's a large meal, they might keep it underwater, using tree roots or rocks to weight it down, like a food store to return to later.

OLD TIMERS

These giants are ancient survivors – they even outlasted the dinosaurs. They had already been walking the Earth for 100 million years by the time the Tyrannosaurus rex came along.

How to stay alive

↑ KEEP YOUR DISTANCE.
You might beat a croc in a marathon, but probably not a sprint. They can explode out of the water at almost 30 kilometres per hour. Stay at least five metres back from the water's edge to avoid them lunging at you.

@ BE UNPREDICTABLE.
If you need to collect water from a river or lake, then change where you collect from each day so they don't learn where to wait for you.

● SWIM DURING THE DAY.
If you have to swim, then make sure the water is clear enough to see the bottom, and avoid swimming at night, dawn or dusk — a croc's favourite times to hunt.

+ EXPECT CROCS EVERYWHERE.
Just because you can't see one, it doesn't mean it's not there. Crocs can hide in knee-deep water and come out onto land. Keep your wits about you.

✱ MIND YOUR LEFTOVERS.
Don't get rid of food scraps in the water — you'll attract crocs to the area and they might want you for dessert.

✓ STICK TO BIGGER BOATS.
Crocs have been known to pull people off kayaks and small boats. Stick with something larger if you want to get on the water.

STATUS

Least concern 🟩🟩🟩🟩

Saltwater crocodiles have been around for 200 million years, but they are starting to disappear in some areas. New buildings cover their home and nesting grounds, and people hunt them for their skins.

Frozen

Living in a land of ice and snow has shaped some of the toughest creatures on the planet. In sub-zero temperatures, it can be dangerous for us humans to simply be outside, but here, it isn't just the cold that bites...

Polar Bear

* **Frozen**
* **Mammal**

camouflage coat

powerful paws!

Very few of the dangerous animals in this book will try to hunt you – but polar bears are one. They are the largest bears on the planet, with paws the size of dinner plates and a paw swipe that could stun a whale. At 800 kilograms, these giants weigh as much as ten men, and if they stand on their back legs, they're twice as tall. They hunt everything from reindeer to seals, and walruses to beluga whales.

Method of attack

Polar bears often hunt on sea ice, where there aren't any trees or bushes to hide behind, so they've got to be super sneaky. If their prey is floating on ice, they can swim underwater to leap out and surprise it. If they smell a seal beneath the snow, they quietly creep closer, before standing up tall and crashing down onto them. Only one in fifty hunts are successful for a polar bear. Imagine if you had to work that hard for a meal!

TRICK OF THE LIGHT

Polar bears aren't actually white. Their skin is black, and their hair is transparent! They just look white because of the way light bounces off their fur.

How to stay alive

- **CHOOSE A LOOKOUT.** Work in shifts to keep an eye out for polar bears while the rest of your group sleeps.

- **DISTANCE YOURSELF FROM FOOD.** Cook and wash your dishes at least a football pitch distance away from where you're sleeping.

- **SET BOUNDARIES.** An electric fence or fence with alarm bells around the camp will warn off the bear and let people know it's coming.

- **FIND AN EXPERT.** Travel with an experienced guide. Ideally someone who is able to carry bear spray if needed.

- **GET AWAY FROM THE SHORE.** Polar bears are normally found on sea ice, or near coastlines. If you want to avoid polar bears, head further inland.

- **STAY HIDDEN IF YOU CAN.** If you see a bear, but it hasn't seen you, stay downwind – so the wind is moving from the polar bear towards you. That way your smell won't move towards its powerful nose.

- **ACT HUMAN.** If a bear has seen you, let it know you're human. While polar bears can hunt humans, they usually try to avoid us. Move upwind so your human smell drifts towards the bear, wave your arms and talk in a low calm voice.

- **GROUP TOGETHER.** If a bear is trying to hunt you, it might follow you, circle you, or simply head straight for you. Group together and make lots of noise. Defend yourself if you have to – aim for the face and nose (but avoid the teeth!).

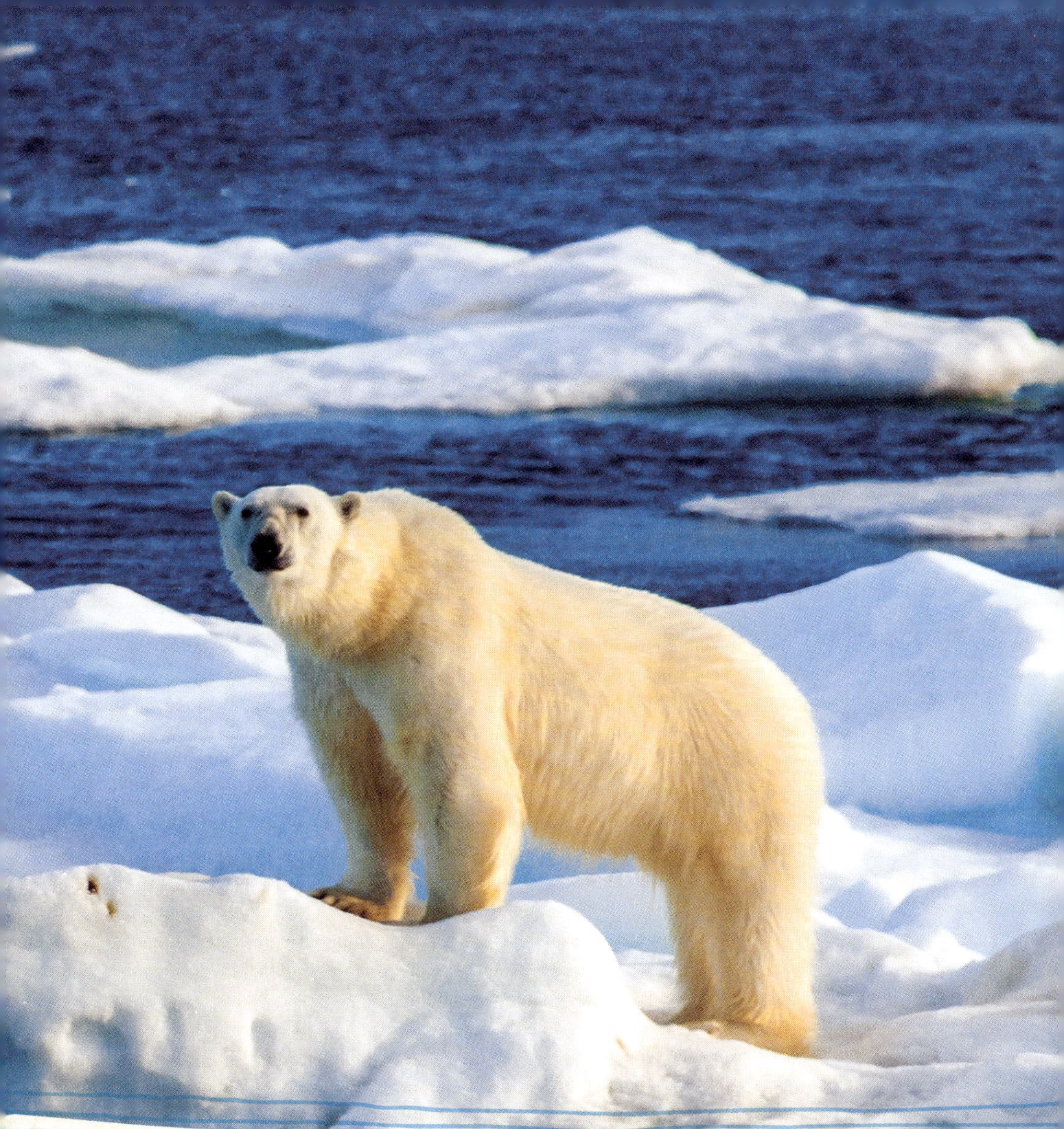

Vulnerable ☐☐☐☐☐

Polar bears live in some of the coldest places on Earth, which makes them hard to study, so we don't really know how they're doing. It's thought there are about 26,000 of them. In some places, their numbers are starting to decrease due to climate change melting the ice they need to hunt on.

Leopard Seal

Frozen

Mammal

spiky teeth

speedy swimmer

Swimming in icy Antarctic waters is enough to chill anyone's bones, especially with a smart, sneaky hunter patrolling the waves. With sleek spotty bodies, leopard seals rocket through the water at 40 kilometres per hour, like penguin-seeking missiles. They have enormous jaws, eating everything from large prey like emperor penguins and Weddell seals, to small prey like squid. Their unusual teeth can even act like a sieve to filter out tiny prey such as plankton. They've sadly also been known to kill people.

Leopard seals are the second largest of the Antarctic seals (after the enormous elephant seal). Females are bigger than males, weighing as much as a polar bear and reaching almost four metres long.

Method of attack

Much like the big cat that shares its name, leopard seals will sneak as close to their prey as possible before going in for the kill. They silently approach as close as they can before relying on their speed and underwater acrobatic skills to catch their target. Their spiky fork-shaped teeth are sharp enough to slice through flesh and bone.

How to stay alive

↓ **STAY ON THE ICE.** It's not wise to spend too long in the freezing cold waters of Antarctica, but especially when there are leopard seals about.

● **WATCH THE EDGE.** Just because you're on the surface doesn't mean you're safe from a leopard seal attack. They have been known to launch onto the ice to capture prey.

✱ **STEER CLEAR OF MUM.** Leopard seal mothers feed their babies milk for just four weeks before they're on their own. Mum can be very protective during this time.

✕ **BLOCK THEM.** Attacks on humans are incredibly rare, but leopard seals are very curious and will often approach anyone in the water. Keep something you don't mind being nibbled between you and them, like a fin or an underwater camera.

STATUS

Least concern

Leopard seals are found throughout the cold Southern Ocean, where humans rarely visit. It's thought melting sea ice might have an impact on them and their prey, but for the moment these powerful predators are doing well.

Southern Elephant Seal

* Frozen
* Mammal

very heavy!

thick blubber

It might not seem like there's much to fear from the enormous brown 'sausages' flopping around on the beaches of the Southern Ocean, but looks can be deceiving. Elephant seals are the biggest seals on the planet. They can reach over six metres long and weigh over 3,700 kilograms. That's up to 60 people!

Elephant seals are usually found far out to sea where they hunt fish and squid deep in the ocean. Every year they come ashore at special times to moult (shed fur and skin), give birth and breed.

Method of attack

In the breeding season, big males like to throw their weight around. One enormous male, called the 'beach master', will fight to the death to keep all the females to himself. Elephant seals can have bloody battles, smashing their chests together and gouging each other with sharp teeth. Losing males become grumpy at missing out and can be aggressive with anyone nearby, including people.

How to stay safe

- **KEEP YOUR DISTANCE.** Elephant seals can move surprisingly quickly on land, at up to ten kilometres per hour. Give yourself a head start by staying away.

- **STEP ASIDE.** Don't expect manners from an elephant seal. Don't stand in front of them. If they're on the move, they won't mind flattening you like a blubbery steamroller.

- **FIND A STICK.** Use a long, strong stick to keep an elephant seal at more than arm's length while you make an exit.

- **STAY OUTSIDE THE HERD.** Elephant seals take up a lot of room – you don't want to get stuck in the middle of a herd.

- **LET THEM FIGHT.** An elephant seal fight can look horrific and can even be deadly. Don't be tempted to break it up, as you might get seriously injured by the super heavyweights.

STATUS

Least concern 🟩🟩🟩🟩

Elephant seals used to be hunted for their blubber when humans discovered that it could be used to make oil. They were close to extinction until they became protected and are now doing well.

Grey Wolf

 Frozen

Mammal

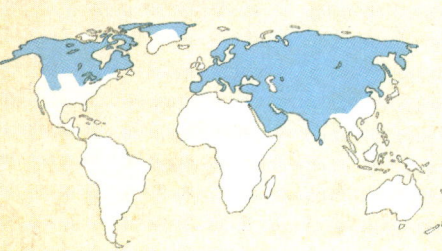

big teeth!

sharp claws

You're out hiking in the wilderness and you hear a familiar sound... a high-pitched howl, followed by others. It's enough to send a chill down anyone's spine. You've arrived in wolf territory!

Grey wolves are very adaptable, living in a variety of habitats – from the frozen High Arctic to dry deserts in the Middle East. They are the largest wild dogs on the planet, about twice as large as your typical pet pooch (but smaller than some massive breeds like Great Danes). These chunky pups are pure meat-eaters (carnivores) and have the teeth to prove it. Their long, sharp canine teeth can be over seven centimetres long, about the length of your little finger – perfect for gripping onto prey and piercing flesh.

Method of attack

Whilst one wolf is dangerous, wolves normally hunt in packs where they become so deadly there is little they can't take down. A wolf pack might have as many as 36 members. The strongest wolf is called the 'alpha male' and his partner is the 'alpha female'. They are usually the only parents of the group and they tell the other wolves what to do by using their voice or body language. Wolves often try to separate one animal from its herd. Taking it in turns at the front, they chase their prey until it's so tired that it can't run any more. Working together, they can bring down prey ten times their size, such as moose. It's very rare, but humans have been killed by wolves.

How to stay alive

✚ **GET ANGRY.** Most of the time, wolves will try to leave you alone, but if they're getting too close, it's time to go on the attack. Throw rocks and sticks. You can even charge towards them but just make sure you don't run away: that's what their prey does.

✱ **GET LOUD!** Shout. Clap. Whistle. Often people hiking in wolf country take an air horn along, which is very loud.

● **HAVE A STARING CONTEST.** Give that wolf your best 'stink eye'. Eye contact shows them you're not scared.

✓ **STICK TOGETHER.** With a few of you together, you're scarier to a wolf. If there are lots of wolves, get back-to-back with your friends so the wolves can't get behind you for a sneak attack.

◉ **SLOWLY RETREAT.** While staring down the wolves, slowly back off to a safe place.

↓ **GET INDOORS.** Get inside the nearest car or house and shut the door.

✓ **CLIMB A TREE.** If you can't get away, then climb a tree. Wolves can't climb and won't be able to follow.

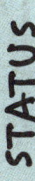

Least concern 🟩🟩🟩🟩

Although wolves are still sometimes hunted by humans, they're so widespread and often in such remote places, that their numbers are generally stable. With better protection in place, these amazing predators are slowly returning to areas where they had once been totally wiped out.

Moose

✳︎ Frozen

 Mammal

impressive antlers

strong hooves

Strutting through their forest kingdoms, these magnificent animals aren't like the deer you read about in storybooks. Moose are the largest deer in the world. These horse-sized beasts can be a whole head taller than a man and weigh up to 700 kilograms. Their enormous antlers can stretch two metres across and have as many as 40 sharp points.

Moose are vegetarian and use their impressive antlers to defend themselves against wolves and bears, or to fight with other moose. They grow a new set of antlers each spring and drop them in winter.

Method of attack

Moose are very protective parents and will charge at any threat to their young, kicking out with their front hooves and lowering their antlers. They can be very grumpy and mostly want to be left alone to graze in peace. It's rare but moose have been known to kill people.

How to stay safe

- ↓ **STAY OUT OF THE WAY.** Even if a moose is blocking your path, just wait patiently and it should move on.

- ✚ **LEARN MOOSE CODE.** An unhappy moose might raise the fur on its shoulder hump, hold its ears back or lick its lips. Time to back off.

- ✓ **RUN AWAY.** If a moose charges, it's okay to run. Unlike bears or lions, moose don't normally chase someone running away. Most of the time, moose 'bluff charge' with a short warning run, but it's best to assume they're serious.

- ✱ **GET SOMETHING BETWEEN YOU.** Try to find something big and solid to put between you, like a large tree or a vehicle.

- ✗ **DON'T FEED THEM.** Moose can seem friendly, but they'll soon get grumpy when the food runs out. You might create a dangerous situation for yourself or someone else.

- ↓ **DROP AND COVER.** If you are knocked to the ground by a moose, curl up into a ball, and cover your head with your hands. Stay still until it has left the area.

STATUS

Least concern

Moose are found across the northern forests of North America, Europe and Asia. Their numbers are increasing with our protection.

Siberian Tiger

✱✱ Frozen

▢ Mammal

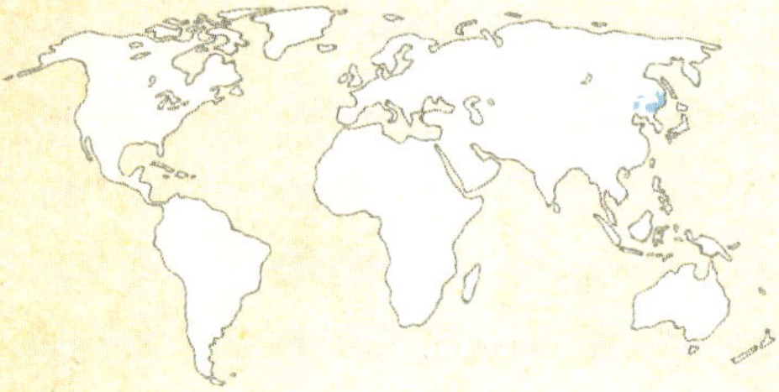

deadly bite

retractable claws

Hidden amongst the snowy forests of far east Russia are the largest cats on Earth: Siberian tigers. They can grow to over three metres long and weigh over 400 kilograms – about 100 times heavier than a house cat! Their stunning black, white and orange stripes provide camouflage amongst the branches and trees of their forest homes.

Siberian tigers mostly hunt deer and wild boar. They use their eyes and ears more than their nose to find prey, and prefer to hunt at night, under cover of darkness. Sharp retractable claws hide inside their large, padded feet, which keep their footsteps quiet.

Method of attack

Siberian tigers stalk their prey, trying to stay hidden as they approach their target. They'll crawl on their belly, hide behind rocks and trees, and even swim to get close without detection. When they're close enough, they can sprint at 80 kilometres per hour, jump on their prey then deliver a deadly bite to the neck.

How to stay alive

✗ **DON'T RUN.** Tigers can run as fast as a car, so you won't win that race, and they will think of you as prey.

✓ **MAKE SOME NOISE.** Snap twigs, shout, clap – but don't scream. The high pitch might sound like an animal in distress and encourage it to hunt.

✱ **MAKE YOURSELF BIG.** Open your jacket. Raise your hands above your head to look big and scary.

✗ **DON'T TURN YOUR BACK.** Tigers often start to approach when they think they can't be seen.

↓ **STAY CALM AND BACK AWAY.** An approaching tiger may just be curious. Back away slowly and drop any clothing or items you have. Hopefully it will inspect them and stop following you.

✗ **DON'T LOOK IT IN THE EYE.** While you want to let it know you're there, looking a tiger in the eye can seem threatening if you accidentally make it a staring contest.

● **READ THE SIGNS.** A tiger hissing, roaring, or with ears flattened back in defensive mode means it wants you to leave. It may be protecting something precious like a kill or cubs. Back away slowly.

✗ **DON'T BE LAST.** Supposedly tigers will often target the stragglers of a walking group. If you're with more experienced guides, take up a position in the middle of the pack.

❗ **DEFEND YOURSELF.** You'll rarely see a tiger hunting you until it's too late. If one is stalking you, make noises, throw rocks and defend yourself if it charges.

STATUS

Endangered 🟧🟧⬜⬜⬜

Being both beautiful and deadly is often a recipe for disaster. Tigers have been hunted by humans for hundreds of years for their stunning fur, but also because of our fear of them. It's thought there are only around 400 Siberian tigers left.

American Bison

* Frozen
* Mammal

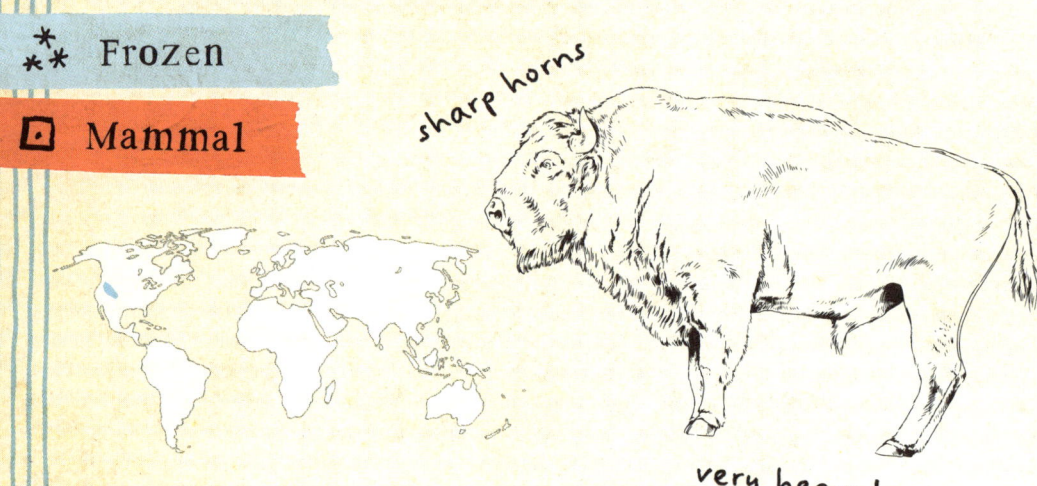

sharp horns

very heavy!

Wandering the great plains of North America, bison might just seem like hairy cattle, but these are their bigger, wilder cousins. Weighing up to 1,000 kilograms and standing taller than a grown man, bison have a bad attitude to match their enormous size. Their horns curl inwards to a sharp point, which they use to stab at any unwelcome threats. They can also run at an impressive 60 kilometres per hour.

When a predator approaches, bison form a defensive circle around their calves, presenting a barricade of horns and hooves towards the attacker. Thanks to their enormous size and weaponry, adult bison don't have many predators.

Method of attack

Bison eat grass, but these vegetarians aren't just defensive. They'll go on the attack if they feel threatened. They put those horns to good use trying to toss, slash and gore any threat — including humans. It's incredibly rare, but bison have been known to kill people.

How to stay safe

- ✓ **DO SOME DETECTIVE WORK.** Look out for trees that have been gored, fresh dung, or footprints that look like two bananas facing each other. That way you'll know bison are about.

- ↓ **KEEP YOUR DISTANCE.** Don't approach closer than 100 metres.

- ✗ **DON'T RUN.** Bison are really fast and startle easily. If you run, they might follow.

- ๏ **READ THE SIGNS.** A grumpy bison will raise and swish its tail; snort and toss its head; paw the ground; or turn around and poo in your direction (charming!).

- ● **WATCH THE HEAD GEAR.** During rutting season (when male bison charge each other to impress females) they will often carry twigs or leaves on their head. This may be a bison looking for a fight.

- ✚ **LOOK OUT FOR MUM.** Never come between a mother and her calf.

STATUS

Near-threatened ▢▢▢▢▢

Bison might seem powerful, but they were no match for humans when we started to hunt them 200 years ago. There used to be 60 million bison all across North America. Now there are just 30,000 wild bison and all are in protected areas.

Wolverine

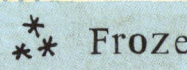
Frozen

Mammal

bone-crushing teeth

long claws

You've probably heard of the superhero, but he's nowhere near as awesome as the real-life wolverine. One of the largest members of the weasel family, they tip the scales at 20 kilograms – and at just over a metre long, they're roughly the size of a dog. That might not sound fearsome, but these creatures are so strong and aggressive that they've been known to bring down prey five times their size, like black bears and moose, with their sharp, bone-crushing teeth.

Method of attack

Wolverines are cold weather specialists and don't seem bothered by snow, even blizzards. They have wide feet with semi-retractable claws for chasing down prey over slippery surfaces. They can run at 15 kilometres per hour for many hours at a time. They've been spotted chasing reindeer for a whopping 60 kilometres until the deer is too exhausted to run anymore and receives a killer bite to the neck.

How to stay safe

- 🌀 **MAKE SOME NOISE.** Wolverines are brave, but not foolish – they'll try to avoid you if they can.

- ✓ **MAKE YOURSELF BIG.** If a wolverine doesn't back off, get your arms up above your head to seem bigger.

- ✗ **AVOID DEAD ANIMALS.** Wolverines are scavengers that feed on dead animals. They may try to defend their food.

- ✓ **BACK AWAY SLOWLY.** Retreat and give the wolverine some space, and it should leave you alone.

- ✚ **KEEP YOUR PETS AWAY.** They might be tempting for a hungry wolverine.

- ✗ **DON'T BE A HERO.** One man was attacked by a wolverine while trying to rescue it from a trap. Better to send in the professionals.

STATUS

Least concern 🟩🟩🟩🟩

Wolverines live in such wild and large areas that they are mostly able to live in peace. However, their numbers are shrinking as their forest homes are being chopped down and roads disturb their hunting grounds.

Arctic Tern

✳︎✳︎ Frozen

◯ Bird

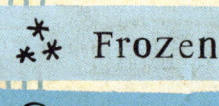

powerful beak!

The stunningly beautiful arctic tern is the most well-travelled animal in the world. Each autumn, this sun-seeker flies from pole to pole to get two summers and avoid winter altogether. Despite their angelic looks, arctic terns are among the most aggressive birds on Earth. They nest together in tightly knit colonies and attack anyone who comes close. Even polar bears can end up injured following some powerful stabs of their beaks.

Method of attack

Arctic terns normally use their sharp beaks for catching fish. They hover about ten metres above the sea surface before diving down to snap up their prey. They do something similar when defending their nests. The males hover above the intruder and stoop down to peck them around the eyes, head and nose. When they all gang together, it's like it's raining daggers.

How to stay safe

- ✓ **KNOW YOUR BIRDS.** Terns have black caps, a forked tail, and red beaks during the breeding season. They nest on flat gravelly areas around June to July, which is when they're extra aggressive.

- ● **AVOID NESTING AREAS.** Let the terns sit on their eggs in peace. It's hard enough having to collect fish for mum without having to worry about a human.

- ✶ **LISTEN UP.** Terns will cry out with a 'keet-keet-keet' sound when you're getting too close.

- ✚ **PROTECT YOUR HEAD.** Sometimes, it's impossible to avoid a tern nest if they settle near where you live. Wear a helmet and put the hood of your coat up to try and keep the beaks at bay.

- ↓ **GET LOW.** Terns seem to attack the highest point on their target, whatever that might be, so hold a stick high above your head. They should attack the stick instead of you. Don't wave it, though, as you might accidentally hurt these incredible birds.

STATUS

Least concern ▢▢▢▢▢

Arctic terns are such good travellers that they are quite happy moving home if they need to avoid a threat. However, a warming world is impossible to escape and has affected some of the food they eat. Their numbers seem to be going down, but fortunately they're a long way off from becoming extinct.

Jungle

In the dark and tangled tropical forests are some of life's great treasures — beautiful, strange, and sometimes deadly. Jungles may be packed with creatures, but with so many places to hide, it can be hard to spot their more dangerous residents.

Green Anaconda

Jungle

Reptile

crushing constrictor!

long fangs

Imagine you're wading through the murky wetlands of South America and suddenly your toe bumps into something as big as a tree trunk... and then it moves. Green anacondas are the largest snakes on Earth. Females are much bigger than males and can reach lengths of nine metres – that's as long as three cars parked end-to-end! Their muscular bodies can be over 30 centimetres thick, and can weigh up to 250 kilograms. They can eat just about anything, from fish to caiman. They are easily large enough to eat humans, but fortunately there are no reports of people being eaten – although many have been attacked.

Method of attack

Anacondas only need to eat every few weeks, so they wait for prey to come to them, then strike with long sharp fangs. Their clever teeth curve backwards, so the more their dinner pulls away, the deeper its teeth sink in. Anacondas are constrictors, which means they coil their body tightly around their prey and squeeze – crushing tighter and tighter until it's no longer possible to breathe at all.

How to stay safe

✓ **RUN.** Anacondas are fast in water, but not so quick out of it. Get out of the water and onto dry land.

✚ **GET THE UPPER HAND.** If an anaconda has bitten you, make sure to keep your arms free: you'll need them to pull it off you.

✱ **HAVE A PARTNER.** Exploring with a friend – or better yet, lots of people – will mean you have help nearby.

◉ **UNWIND FROM THE BOTTOM.** If you have a hand free, then grab the end of the anaconda's tail and start to unwind it. The anaconda's tight squeeze relies on gripping against itself, and if you unwind it, it will quickly loosen.

STATUS

Least concern

Green anacondas are widespread in the tropical wetlands of South America and often live in places that are hard for humans to reach – which is good for them. Their homes have some threats – like dams and oil drilling – but for now they're doing alright.

Poison Dart Frog

- ☼ **Jungle**
- ▽ **Amphibian**

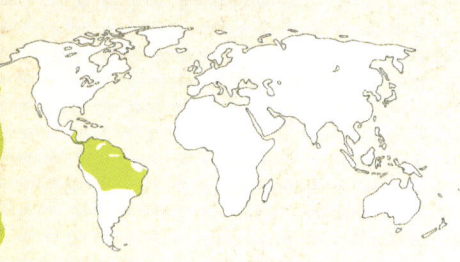

brightly coloured

toxic skin

Hopping through the humid forests of Central and South America are some of the most beautiful frogs on the planet. While they could fit in the palm of your hand, it wouldn't be a good idea to hold one – their skin is covered in a deadly poison. Local tribes, like the Choco and Naonama people of Colombia, rub their hunting darts all over the frog's skin before firing them through blow pipes to kill their targets. That's why they're known as poison dart frogs. One frog has enough poison on its tiny body to kill anywhere from ten to a hundred people.

Method of attack

Being brightly coloured is the main defensive warning sign for poison dart frogs and means 'back off'. If that doesn't work, they can stick their bottoms in the air and wave their brightly coloured bodies around to really make their point. If a predator tries to eat them, they will quickly spit them back out again as the poison makes them swell up, feel sick, or stops their muscles working.

How to stay alive

✗ **DON'T PICK THEM UP.** That's a good rule for most frogs as our hands can pass on disease, burn them or dry them out. With poison dart frogs, the danger definitely goes both ways.

✗ **DON'T CHECK FOR PRINCES.** If you're thinking about kissing a frog, think again. Once their poison hits your saliva, you'll be in deadly trouble.

✓ **COVER OPEN WOUNDS.** Poison becomes deadly when it gets into your blood, so make sure you get a plaster over any cuts or grazes. That's also a good idea in tropical parts of the world where it can be easy to get an infection in any wounds.

YOU ARE WHAT YOU EAT

The poison on a dart frog's body comes from the toxic ants and mites they eat. When fed something else, they're no longer poisonous.

STATUS

Varied 🟥⬜🟧⬜🟩

There are almost 200 different kinds of poison dart frogs, each facing different challenges. Some are close to extinction because of their forest homes shrinking. Many are under threat from the deadly 'chytrid' (pronounced kit-rid) fungus that is threatening frogs worldwide. Some, fortunately, are doing just fine.

Southern Cassowary

- Jungle
- Bird

two metres tall!

huge claws

The remote jungles of New Guinea and Northern Australia are stalked by one of the biggest, strangest and most dangerous birds on the planet. At almost two metres tall, the southern cassowary can easily look you in the eye. Females are bigger than males and can grow to over 50 kilograms. That's heavy enough to keep these flightless birds permanently on the ground. Instead of flying, they walk around on two enormous feet, which are their greatest weapon, as each has a ten-centimetre long, dagger-like claw.

Although they look menacing, southern cassowaries are normally shy and will try to avoid danger when they can. These colourful giants mostly eat fallen fruit but will sometimes eat bugs and mushrooms. They're wonderful (and protective) parents, with dad doing most of the work sitting on eggs and looking after the chicks.

Method of attack

Cassowaries are known to be aggressive and, when threatened, they can charge at up to 50 kilometres per hour. They use their sharp beak and helmeted head to attack, but it's their feet that are really dangerous: their stabbing claws will kick and slash, trying to cause maximum damage. While serious injuries are rare, there have been extreme cases where people have died.

How to stay alive

 LISTEN UP. Although they move silently, cassowaries make a powerful, low roar which will give you an early warning that they're nearby. It sounds a bit like a motorbike starting up.

LEAVE THE AREA. Generally, cassowaries don't immediately start on the attack. If you see a cassowary, just give them space and get out of their way.

 WATCH OUT FOR CHICKS. Cassowaries defend their chicks fiercely, so they might be more likely to attack when their young are nearby.

✗ **DON'T FEED THEM.** Feeding cassowaries can mean they'll expect meals, and they'll get grumpy when food doesn't appear.

 READ THE SIGNS. A threatened cassowary will fluff out its feathers to appear larger, and its colourful head and the dangly bits of their neck (known as a 'wattle') may become brighter.

 MOVE TO SHELTER. Cassowaries are fast, and might chase you, but it's best just to get away even if they aren't. Find a car or building, or get behind a fence.

✓ **LEAVE THEM BE.** Cassowaries are big animals, and their fluffy feathers offer excellent protection so it's not worth fighting back. They are more likely to cause you harm than the other way around.

 DON'T PLAY DEAD. Often, people who have suffered serious injuries were lying down or curled in a ball. Unlike some animals, cassowaries won't stop their attack.

Least concern ▨▨▨▢▢

STATUS

There are thought to be around 40,000 southern cassowaries left, enough not to worry about extinction any time soon. However, that number is dropping as their forest home shrinks to make way for increasing numbers of people. They are also hunted for meat.

Bullet Ant

- Jungle
- Invertebrate

large mandibles

three centimetres long!

In the forests of Central and South America, you might be on the lookout for jaguars and snakes, but sometimes it's the smaller creatures you need to watch. At three centimetres long, bullet ants are almost as long as your thumb. That might not sound big – but in the ant world, that's giant. They have a chunky head, a thin middle and a big bottom with a large stinger.

Worker ants spend all day climbing up into the treetops or combing the forest floor, looking for bugs to hunt and bring back to the nest. They aren't aggressive, but will quickly defend themselves, their nest and their queen.

Method of attack

When bullet ants find an intruder attacking their nest (or someone accidentally stepping on it), they swarm into action. They let out a little alarm sound and start stinging anything they can reach. Their sting is agony, and the pain can last for 24 hours.

SERIOUS STINGER

One brave scientist called Justin Schmidt allowed himself to be stung by every kind of stinging insect to decide which was most painful. Bullet ants came out on top. He described their sting as 'like walking over flaming charcoal with a three-inch nail embedded in your heel.'

How to stay safe

- **LOOK OUT FOR THE LITTLE THINGS.** In a noisy forest, it can be easy to get distracted. Stay alert to the smaller creatures, too.

- **SUIT UP.** This is no time for looking fashionable. Wear chunky boots, long socks and tuck your trousers into them – anything to keep the ants from your skin.

- **MIND YOUR STEP.** Make sure you can see where you're putting your feet as you walk.

- **KNOW YOUR NESTS.** Bullet ants usually nest underground at the base of large trees. You should see a hole and ants coming and going – not a good place to sit for a picnic.

STATUS

Unknown
☐ ? ☐ ? ☐

Scientists don't have an accurate idea of how many bullet ants there are. However, as their forest home is shrinking, it's likely that their numbers are dropping too.

Amazonian Giant Centipede

- Jungle
- Invertebrate

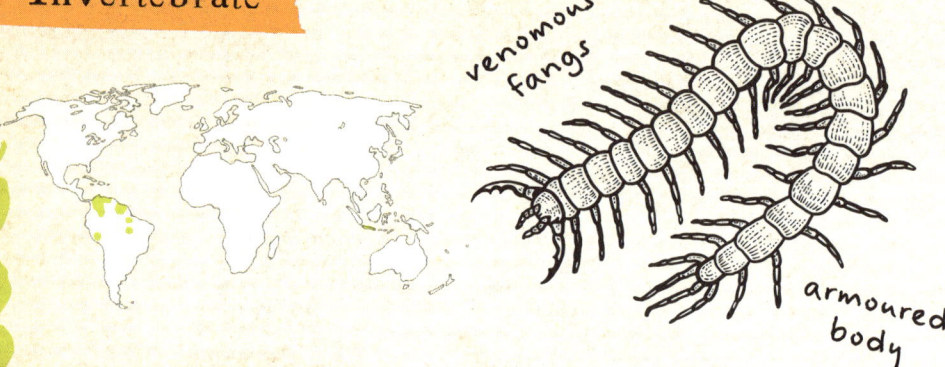

In the humid jungles of South America, an armoured predator charges through the undergrowth, taking down everything from tarantulas and frogs, to mice and bats. The Amazonian giant centipede is fearsome. Over 30 centimetres long, they could have their front legs on your knee while their back legs are on the ground! Speaking of legs, they have 42 or 46 sharp, spiny legs to scuttle around on. Despite 'centipede' literally meaning 100-footed, few, if any, have exactly 100 feet.

Method of attack

Centipedes don't have great vision, so at night they stalk around with their long antennae held out in front of them, trying to detect prey. Their back legs are also built like long feelers and point out behind them, meaning they don't miss their prey whichever way it comes. Once they find their target, they coil around it like a snake and drive their sharp venomous fangs deep into the victim's body.

How to stay safe

✓ **WEAR HIGH BOOTS.** If you're walking in centipede territory, wear boots tall enough to avoid a bite to the skin.

↑ **HANG UP CLOTHES AND SHOES.** Centipedes are great climbers, but this should reduce the chance of them sleeping in your slippers!

◉ **SLEEP INSIDE A SEALED MOSQUITO NET.** If the idea of sharing a bed with a centipede creeps you out, then get a mosquito net that you can zip yourself into. Just make sure you're alone in it first!

✓ **TUCK IN YOUR BEDSHEETS.** If your bedsheets are touching the floor, then it's easy for bugs to climb up.

✚ **TIDY UP.** Centipedes love clutter, so leave them nowhere to hide.

✱ **CARRY A POWERFUL TORCH.** Giant centipedes hate the light and will try to get away from it.

● **CHECK OPEN DRINK CANS.** Reportedly, someone was killed when they drank from a can where a centipede was hiding.

STATUS

Unknown ☐ ? ☐ ? ☐

It's very hard to keep track of bug numbers because they are relatively small and well hidden, but it's believed these giant centipedes are doing just fine. They are even popular with some of the local people because they kill pests like mice and locusts.

Chimpanzee

- Jungle
- Mammal

super smart!

seriously strong

Chimpanzees are intelligent and complicated creatures, just like us. They have different and changing friendship groups. If they get hurt, they know which plants provide medicine. They build comfy beds to sleep in at night. It's no wonder we find them so interesting. However, forget dangers like claws and fangs – a big brain is the thing to watch out for.

Chimpanzees can team up to form dangerous gangs. Although they're slightly smaller than we are, they are much stronger than us. You'd be strong, too, if you spent all day doing gymnastics and climbing in the treetops! They will hunt all kinds of creatures and are smart enough to make tools and weapons. They use long thin twigs for collecting ants and make spears and clubs for killing bigger animals. Chimps have been known to kill and eat each other, and in extreme cases even attack and kill people.

Method of attack

Chimps will wait for a good moment to attack, when they can surprise their target or outnumber them. A large group will often attack lone animals. With tearing arms, punching fists and a fierce bite, they'll aim for the face, hands and feet.

HAIRY COUSIN

They might look quite different, but scientists believe chimpanzees are our closest animal relatives. We had the same great-great-great- (keep saying great for a very long time) grandparent, who would have lived about 10 million years ago.

How to stay safe

✓ **KEEP YOUR DISTANCE.**
Wild chimpanzees will rarely attack humans provided you give them some space.

WATCH THE HAIR.
If a chimp's hair is standing on end, that probably means it's excited or scared. Best to back off.

LEARN THE LANGUAGE.
Chimpanzees make sounds, pull faces and wave their arms around to let you know what they're thinking. If a chimp wants to play, it might smile with its top lip covering its teeth. If it's frightened, it might do a wide smile, baring its gums.

KEEP AN EYE OUT.
Don't let a chimp surprise you; keep close watch.

✗ **DON'T FEED THEM.**
It might seem cute to pack a spare banana snack for your wild cousin, but if chimps think humans should be giving them food, then it might lead to an attack.

✗ **BEWARE OF PETS.**
Chimpanzees do NOT make good pets, and, in some ways, pet chimps are more dangerous than wild chimps. Many chimp attacks have happened from pets that have had enough.

STATUS

Endangered ■■□□□

Chimpanzees are, sadly, on the edge of extinction for lots of reasons: they get hunted for their meat; are caught to be sold as pets or zoo animals; humans are chopping down their forests; and we are even spreading some of our diseases to them.

Tarantula

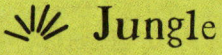
Jungle

Invertebrate

very fast!

deadly fangs

They're enormous. They're hairy. They have big fangs. For many people, tarantulas are the ultimate spider nightmare. For others, they're popular pets. There are over a thousand different kinds of tarantulas, found all around the world, and they each bring different dangers.

The largest is the goliath bird-eating tarantula, weighing as much as three chicken eggs, with legs up to 28 centimetres across. As its name suggests, it can tackle prey as big as birds with its powerful bite and two-centimetre-long fangs. Strangely, one of the main dangers is its kick. Some tarantulas have sharp hook-like hairs on their tummy. When threatened, they kick these hairs off, which float through the air like an angry cloud. They can cause itching, rashes and blisters, as well as damaging your eyes and lungs.

While most tarantulas have a fairly harmless venom, less painful than a bee sting, the venom of the gooty sapphire tarantula is one of the worst. It's very painful, can make you feel sick and can give you muscle cramps that last for hours, or even days.

Method of attack

Tarantulas are usually ambush predators, waiting inside their silky burrows for prey to come past. When their target gets within striking distance, they can move incredibly quickly. They wrap their legs around their victim and scoop them towards their sharp and deadly fangs.

COLOURFUL CREATURES

Tarantulas can come in all shapes, sizes and colours. This gooty sapphire ornamental tarantula (also called the peacock tarantula) is a breathtaking blue!

How to stay safe

✓ **KEEP YOUR EYES PEELED FOR TREASURE.** Tarantulas' eyes shine like sparkly little diamonds in torchlight. Use that to spot them on the forest floor.

↓ **KEEP YOUR DISTANCE.** Tarantulas are fascinating but stay at least a metre away. If they start kicking hairs, leave the area.

● **WATCH FOR HOLES.** Be careful around any holes in the ground, especially if you can see silk in them: it might be home to a tarantula.

◉ **STICK TO DAYLIGHT HOURS.** If you want to avoid them altogether, then don't go out after dark. Most tarantulas are nocturnal – they are only active at night.

✚ **DRESS CAREFULLY.** Before you put on your shoes, socks and clothes, it's worth giving them a quick check and a shake in case you've had a night-time visitor.

✗ **DON'T PICK THEM UP.** Whilst it might seem a brave or impressive thing to do, there's really no need to pick a tarantula up. Even if it doesn't bite you, you'll probably just stress it out.

STATUS

Varied 🟥⬜🟨⬜🟩

Tarantulas face different threats around the world but many of them are seeing their forest homes shrink or disappear completely. Some are critically endangered, which means they are almost extinct.

Jaguar

- Jungle
- Mammal

camouflage coat

biiiiiiig cat!

The jaguar is beautiful but deadly. Its fur has dark patches on it called rosettes that look like flowers, but you wouldn't want to get close enough to sniff them! Weighing up to 120 kilograms, they're heavier than most adult humans, making them the biggest cats in the Americas. Unlike most cats, this one doesn't mind water. In fact, they can even hunt caiman. They'll also eat animals like tortoises, armadillos and deer. A jaguar's roar sounds like a saw chopping wood, so listen up if you're in their home range.

Method of attack

Jaguars are ambush predators – they jump out and surprise their prey. They rely on their excellent camouflage to stay hidden, and creep silently until they are close enough to pounce. They have the most powerful bite of any of the big cats.

BLACK CATS

Sometimes jaguars are born with very dark fur. These cats are known as black panthers.

How to stay alive

✓ **STAY CALM.** Like lions, running or screaming can make a jaguar go into hunt mode.

↓ **BACK AWAY SLOWLY.** Keep facing the jaguar and slowly back away without making sudden movements.

+ **MAKE YOURSELF LOOK BIGGER.** Raise your arms or open your jacket to appear larger if the jaguar approaches. Maybe grab a branch to wave.

↑ **GET ON AN ADULT'S SHOULDERS.** With two of you, one on top of the other, you'll look like a scary giant to a jaguar!

◎ **BEWARE OF SWIMMING CATS.** If you see one swimming, keep your distance. You might think a jaguar in the water is safe to approach but this is one shipmate you definitely don't want on board!

STATUS

Near-threatened ■ ■ ■ ■ ☐

These cats used to live as far north as the United States, but their home began to shrink as humans spread out. Now they mostly survive in the dense jungles of Central and South America, like the Amazon and the Pantanal. Sadly, even these jungles are disappearing fast as people cut them down to make way for farms.

Gorilla

- Jungle
- Mammal

Gorillas are the largest primates on Earth. These impressive apes can weigh three times as much as an adult human, and might be ten to twenty times as strong – able to lift up to 450 kilograms. They might be vegetarian, but with a bite strength similar to that of a bull shark, you don't want to get on the wrong side of them. The strongest male in the group is the silverback and he's fiercely protective of his family. He'll beat his chest loudly to warn others of his size and strength.

Method of attack

Generally gentle giants, gorillas can show incredible ferocity when threatened. A charging gorilla can reach speeds of 40 kilometres per hour, about as fast as an Olympic sprinter. They can crush bamboo with their bare hands, pull down trees, and drag people around if they feel threatened.

GIGGLING GORILLAS

Just like humans, gorillas love to laugh when playing.

How to stay alive

- **+ KEEP YOUR DISTANCE.** Stay at least seven metres away at all times.
- **✗ NEVER SURROUND A GORILLA.** Make sure the gorilla has an exit route, or it might think you're attacking them.
- **● DON'T LOOK A GORILLA IN THE EYES.** Gorillas hate eye contact and find it threatening.
- **✓ STAY QUIET.** Gorillas use up to 16 different sounds to talk to one another. If you don't speak 'gorilla' (which I'm guessing you don't!), you might say the wrong thing and they will attack!
- **✗ DO NOT RUN.** It can trigger a chase. Stay still or back away slowly.
- **✗ DON'T TOUCH A GORILLA.** You might not have much choice if a youngster decides it wants to come and play with you, but mum and dad will be watching. They might attack if they think you're a threat to their young.

STATUS

Critically endangered ■ ☐ ☐ ☐ ☐

Sadly, a lot of gorillas are killed by people. Sometimes their body parts are sold as medicine (which doesn't work), and sometimes they're hunted for meat. The forests they rely on for food are being cut down to make way for farmland, and for mining metals that are good for making smartphones.

King Cobra

☀ **Jungle**

/// **Reptile**

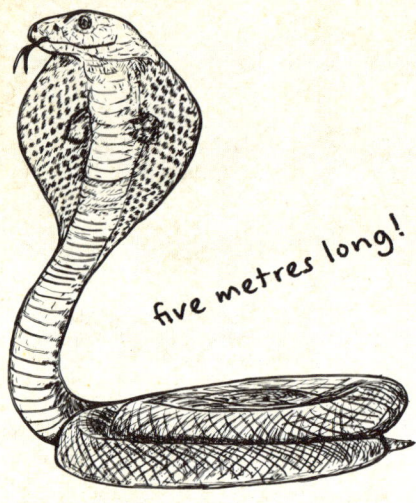

fierce fangs

five metres long!

Imagine you're walking through the jungles of Southern Asia. It's hot. It's sweaty. You turn a corner, and there is a snake so long and so powerful that when it rears up, its head is higher than yours. It lets out a loud hiss that's almost like a growl. It flares out the hood on its neck to appear even larger, and it's not backing off... Meet the king cobra, the largest venomous snake in the world!

These beasts can be more than five metres long, the length of three people lying down. King cobras are very impressive-looking snakes, their colours can vary between olive-green, glimmering yellow, and brown or black, with piercing golden eyes. Beautiful but deadly.

Method of attack

Most snakes this size would be constrictors, squeezing their prey to death, but not the king cobra. Its bite packs enough venom to topple an elephant, let alone a human, though it's actually more likely to prey on other snakes. It stalks them through the undergrowth before delivering a fast and deadly bite as near to their head as possible, to avoid them biting back. There's a reason it's the king!

BIG BAD BITER

The king cobra's venom isn't as strong as the inland taipan's (see page 100), but it makes much more of it. It can inject you with enough venom to fill an egg cup. That's enough to kill 20 people!

How to stay alive

🌀 **FREEZE, THEN BACK AWAY SLOWLY.** Flinching or running away can trigger a snake to strike in confusion. Freezing gives you both time to figure out your next move, and for you, that's simply backing away!

↑ **KEEP A SAFE DISTANCE, THEN DOUBLE IT.** King cobras are very long and very fast. It can be hard to judge how far they can reach. If you do want to keep an eye on one, do it from a long way off.

✓ **STOMP YOUR FEET AS YOU WALK.** Snakes feel vibrations through the ground with their jawbones, in a similar way to how our ears work with sounds in the air. With enough warning stomps, a king cobra shouldn't be surprised to see you and should clear off before you even get close.

✗ **AVOID THEIR NESTS.** King cobras are the only snakes who build nests for their eggs and the female will often stay with them for months. You don't want to anger a protective mother!

● **WEAR A SHIRT OR A HAT.** Usually, king cobras will get out of your way, but sometimes they can hold their ground or go on the attack. Throwing a shirt or hat down in their path will give them something to strike while you back off.

STATUS

Vulnerable 🟨🟨🟨⬜⬜

King cobras usually live in forests and scrubland. Many of their habitats are being chopped down to make way for farms and towns. They are also illegally caught to sell to zoos and for people to have as pets. They're often hunted for food, for their beautiful skin, or for use as medicine. A sad end for an incredible animal.

177

Wild Weapons

In the wild, every creature has its own special toolkit to get a meal or avoid being eaten. Across the animal kingdom are a dazzling number of different tools to bite, pin, crush, sting, slice, pierce and grab.

WILD WEAPONS

Teeth

Teeth make excellent weapons; they're used for biting and killing prey, and chopping up food. They are also one of the oldest wild weapons, first appearing in fish about 500 million years ago before reptiles, birds and mammals even existed. Many teeth (including yours) are coated in something called enamel. It's one of the hardest things in nature, strong enough to bite through bone.

- The teeth of barracuda, angler fish and snakes are long, thin and sharp like needles – ideal for catching on to small, fast-moving prey and not letting go.

- The triangular teeth of great white sharks are serrated, which means they have a zig-zag edge like a saw or a steak knife. This can chop through thick bone and flesh of enormous prey, like whales.

- Lions and saltwater crocodiles need sharp but chunky teeth to be able to bring down massive, struggling prey without breaking.

180

Longest

A contender for the longest tooth is the narwhal. If it was pointing straight up, a narwhal's tooth would be as high as a basketball hoop. The 'unicorn of the sea' has one extraordinary tooth that spirals out of the top of its head and grows into a straight, pointy tusk. You might think it would be a good spear for stabbing prey, but narwhals have recently been filmed using them like a baseball bat, swinging them at fish to stun them.

Razor sharp

If you were brave (or silly!) enough to look into a Komodo dragon's mouth, you might notice a thin line of orange along the edge of their sharp, jagged teeth. They haven't been eating stringy cheese – that orange line is iron, a kind of metal that is perfect for keeping them razor sharp. Metal teeth! Who knew there was such a thing?

Largest

The largest teeth in the animal kingdom belong to the African elephant – their tusks! These massive teeth grow outside of their mouth, either side of their trunk, and can stretch down to the ground. Up to three metres long, they can weigh as much as an adult human. They're used for everything from pushing down trees, to digging for water, as well as fighting each other and defending themselves from predators.

WILD WEAPONS

Claws

Used as defensive slashers by sloth bears, as killing daggers by peregrine falcons, as demolition digits by giant armadillos, and climbing crampons by leopards – claws are the ultimate multi-tool. Claws are long, special nails that grow at the end of some animals' toes, and they have been around for hundreds of millions of years. Claws are so useful they appear all over the animal kingdom.

Longest

- The longest ever claws belonged to a dinosaur called Therizinosaurus. This strange looking animal was ten metres tall, with a huge bottom and short legs, but its strangest features were its claws. At almost a metre long, they would have looked very frightening, but scientists think they were too flimsy to be used for fighting or hunting.

- Today, the longest claws belong to the giant armadillo. Their curved blades can reach up to 20 centimetres long, and they're incredibly thick and strong. They have to be as the armadillo uses them to tear its way into termite mounds which can be as hard as concrete.

Peekaboo!

Some claws are 'retractable', meaning they can pop out when needed, and shrink back into folds of skin afterwards, preventing them from getting blunted on the ground when walking around. Domestic cats and lions both have claws like this, but not all cats do. Cheetahs have short, blunt claws that always poke out a bit. This means when they run, their claws dig into the earth and give them grip, allowing them to reach speeds of 120 kilometres per hour.

Terrifying talons

- Talons are just another name for sharp claws found on some birds, particularly birds of prey. Unlike other predators' claws, which are mainly used to grab hold of prey before delivering a fatal bite, talons are often used as the killing tool. They can be so pin-sharp that they can slice through flesh as easily as butter.

- One contender for the most powerful talons is the harpy eagle. At ten centimetres long, its talons are the same length as a bear's claws, and it has a grip twice as powerful as a dog's bite. The sloths and monkeys that it preys on don't stand a chance!

WILD WEAPONS

Stings

A sting is the sneakiest of the wild weapons as it combines a sharp needle-like point with a painful, or even deadly, dose of venom. Stings are such a useful weapon that they appear all over the animal kingdom, as well as in many plants. At some point in your life, you're likely to be on the receiving end of one.

A painful point

One of the most painful stings on Earth belongs to the tarantula hawk – an enormous wasp that hunts tarantulas with its seven-millimetre sting. Their sting paralyses the spider so that it can't move, and then the wasp lays its eggs inside it, becoming a living meal for the baby hawks when they hatch. Their sting is so painful that one scientist said the only sensible reaction is to lie on the ground and scream.

A million stings

Jellyfish have tiny stings on their tentacles that fire out little venomous harpoons when touched. Their stings are hooked and get stuck in your skin. A lion's mane jellyfish has tentacles that can stretch over 30 metres long, covered in millions of stings.

A sting in the tail

Stingrays have a large sting, usually halfway along their tail, which is shaped like a long, jagged knife with venom leaking out of it. A giant freshwater stingray has a sting up to 38 centimetres long – longer than most school rulers! They only use it for defence if they're caught or stepped on, but it's certainly dangerous enough to kill. It's best to shuffle your feet if you're walking in stingray territory, so you don't step on their back.

Stinging spurs

It's very rare for mammals to sting, but there are some that can. Male platypuses have sharp little hooks on their ankles, known as spurs, which are packed with venom. They use them to sting their opponents when they're fighting. Not only is it incredibly painful for humans, but it is so unusual that many of our painkilling medicines don't work against it.

WILD WEAPONS

Beaks

Pecking, stabbing, slashing, snipping – a beak is quite a weapon. Beaks are made from jaw bones covered in keratin (the same stuff you find in horns and fingernails), making them very strong and tough. The most well-known owners of beaks are birds, who started to evolve them around 66 million years ago, leaving teeth in the past.

Big beaks

▼ The Australian pelican is the owner of the longest beak in the world – almost 50 centimetres long. These big birds practically have fishing nets for mouths, with a large, floppy pouch beneath their beaks that can hold whole fish, turtles and even seagulls.

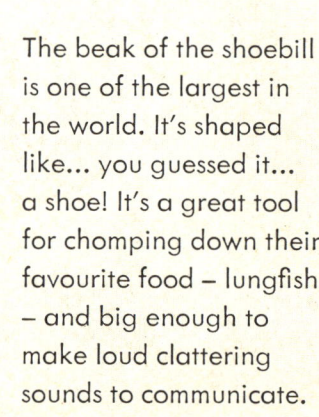

▼ The beak of the shoebill is one of the largest in the world. It's shaped like... you guessed it... a shoe! It's a great tool for chomping down their favourite food – lungfish – and big enough to make loud clattering sounds to communicate.

Sweet tooth

The sword-billed hummingbird might sound like a menacing beast. At 13 centimetres long, it is very large for a hummingbird, but its extraordinary beak can grow just as long. It's not for sword fighting, but for reaching nectar at the bottom of long thin flowers.

Home builder

Woodpeckers have a long, sharp beak that you can hear from miles away. They use it to hammer away at trees, to tell other birds to back off, as well as to drill holes big enough to nest in and raise their chicks.

Helmet head

Beaks can also be great protection. They don't bleed or have a lot of feeling in them, so they make good tools for dangerous activities. The beaks of helmeted hornbills have a large bump like a helmet called a 'casque'. They fly at each other and collide head-first, like battling musk ox.

Other beaks

It isn't just birds that have evolved beaks. Turtles and tortoises have sharp bills for chopping soft plants and animal prey. Cephalopods, like squid and octopus, have sharp snapping beaks like parrots. They are the only hard part of these rubbery animals.

WILD WEAPONS

Muscles

Sometimes, to get food or defend yourself, you don't need brains, venom or complicated body parts – you just need to flex some muscle. Muscles are made up of thousands of tiny string-like fibres that can stretch or squash when your brain tells them to contract. If you try to touch your shoulder with your hand, you'll feel your bicep muscle get shorter and fatter. When you get large bundles of these fibres together, you end up with big muscles and powerful actions, strong enough to kill.

Big and bulky

The strongest animals on land are African elephants. Although they can have huge tusks, their sheer strength and size are their greatest weapons. They're able to flip cars, push down trees, and throw animals as large as rhinos around with their muscular trunk.

Constrictors

Being squeezed to death is the ultimate muscle menace, and that's exactly what snakes like anacondas and constrictors do. Coiling tightly around their prey, they squeeze harder and harder until their prey can't breathe or get blood to their brain.

Coconut crusher

One of the strongest and biggest crabs on Earth is the coconut crab. They can lift up to 30 kilograms – roughly the same weight as a ten-year-old child. Their powerful pincers are built for crushing coconuts and are as strong as a lion's bite.

Serious splash

The most powerful action of any animal belongs to the whales. Humpback whales are able to launch themselves clear of the water. Getting 40 tonnes of whale into the air is the ultimate flex in weightlifting. What goes up, must come down. The massive splash lets everyone know just how big and powerful they are. They've been known to capsize boats and land on top of kayakers.

Strong suckers

The giant pacific octopus is the largest octopus in the world – growing to around 50 kilograms, and sometimes far larger. They have brilliant brains and a sharp beak, but it's their strong arms which are their greatest weapons. They can spread wide enough to hug a car and each of their eight arms is covered in hundreds of strong suction cups. This makes them great weightlifters and powerful enough to overpower sharks.

INDEX OF ANIMALS

African Elephant 24–27
African Lion 12–15
Alligator Snapping Turtle 50–51
Amazonian Giant Centipede 160–161
American Bison 142–143
Arctic Tern 146–147
Banded Sea Krait 70–73
Black Rhino 16–17
Box Jellyfish 62–65
Brown Bear 32–35
Bullet Ant 158–159
Cattle 28–31
Chimpanzee 162–165
Deathstalker Scorpion 88–91
Dromedary Camel 108–109
Electric Eel 76–79
Gila Monster 114–117
Giraffe 22–23
Gorilla 172–173
Great Barracuda 60–61
Great White Shark 52–55
Green Anaconda 150–151
Grey Wolf 132–135
Hippopotamus 18–21
Honey Badger 40–41

Inland Taipan 100–103
Jaguar 170–171
Jumbo Squid 66–69
King Cobra 174–177
Leopard Seal 128–129
Moose 136–137
Mosquito 36–39
Orca 82–85
Ostrich 46–47
Peacock Mantis Shrimp 74–75
Poison Dart Frog 152–153
Polar Bear 124–127
Red Kangaroo 96–99
Red-bellied Piranha 80–81
Saltwater Crocodile 118–121
Saw-scaled Viper 110–113
Siberian Tiger 138–141
Six-eyed Sand Spider 92–95
Southern Cassowary 154–157
Southern Elephant Seal 130–131
Stonefish 56–59
Tarantula 166–169
Tick 42–45
Vampire Bat 104–107
Wolverine 144–145

Published by Collins
An imprint of HarperCollins Publishers
1 Robroyston Gate, Glasgow G33 1JN

collins.co.uk

HarperCollins Publishers
Macken House, 39/40 Mayor Street Upper,
Dublin 1, Ireland D01 C9W8

First published 2026

© HarperCollins Publishers 2026
Collins® is a registered trademark of HarperCollins Publishers Ltd
Text © Sam Hume 2026

Images:
p4(all): Sam Hume. p66: Amanda Cotton. p67(t): robertharding. p67(b): Blue Planet Archive LLC. p68: WaterFrame. p69: Nature Picture Library. p78: Amazon-Images MBSI. p80: imageBROKER.com. p94: Papilio. p105(t): Joe Austin Photography. p182: Nature Picture Library. All other images & illustrations © Shutterstock.

Publisher: Michelle I'Anson
Editor: Beth Rogers
Designers: James Hunter & Kevin Robbins
Cover: James Hunter
Typesetter: QBS
Editorial: Evangeline Sellers, Shelley Welsh & Julianna Dunn
Production: Ilaria Rovera

All rights reserved. No part of this publication may be reproduced, stored in a retrieval system, or transmitted, in any form or by any means, electronic, mechanical, photocopying, recording or otherwise without the prior permission in writing of the publisher and copyright owners.

Without limiting the exclusive rights of any author, contributor or the publisher of this publication, any unauthorised use of this publication to train generative artificial intelligence (AI) technologies is expressly prohibited. HarperCollins also exercise their rights under Article 4(3) of the Digital Single Market Directive 2019/790 and expressly reserve this publication from the text and data mining exception.

The contents of this publication are believed correct at the time of printing. Nevertheless the publisher can accept no responsibility for errors or omissions, changes in the detail given or for any expense or loss thereby caused.

A catalogue record for this book is available from the British Library.

ISBN 978-0-00-875188-3

Printed by Replika Press Pvt. Ltd, India

10 9 8 7 6 5 4 3 2 1

This book contains FSC™ certified paper and other controlled sources to ensure responsible forest management.

For more information visit: www.harpercollins.co.uk/green